Mammals of Colorado

Field Guide

by Stan Tekiela

Adventure Publications
Cambridge, Minnesota

To my wife, Katherine, and daughter, Abigail, with all my love

Acknowledgments

A heartfelt thanks to Wayne and Diane Johnston, who greatly helped me obtain photos for this book. Special thanks to the National Wildlife Refuge System along with state and local agencies, both public and private, for stewarding the lands that are critical to the many mammal species that we love so much.

Edited by Sandy Livoti

Cover and book design by Jonathan Norberg

Silhouettes, tracks and range maps by Anthony Hertzel

Photo credits by photographer and page number:

Cover photo: Mountain Goat by Stan Tekiela

Roger W. Barbour: 58, 65 (Southern), 177 (Yellow-faced) **David J. Behmer**: 96, 98 (inset) **Troy L. Best/ASM***: 98 (main) **Rick and Nora Bowers**: 77 (Mexican), 90 (Pipistrelle, Brazilian), 91 (California, Townsend's, Long-legged, Cave, Free-tailed), 106 (all), 108, 110 (main, top and bottom insets), 114 (top inset), 148, 156, 158 (all), 177 (Botta's), 222, 224 (main), 240, 266, 268 (all) **Kathy Adams Clark/KAC***: 118 **Mary Clay/DPA***: 217, 272 **E. R. Degginger/DPA***: 270 **Larry Ditto/KAC***: 320 (main) **Phil A. Dotson/PRI***: 60, 248 (main) **R. B. Forbes/ASM***: 62 (Bushy-tailed), 65 (Mexican) **Gerald C. Kelley/PRI***: 248 (inset) **Gary Kramer**: 112, 114 (bottom inset), 320 (middle inset) **Stephen J. Krasemann/PRI***: 238 **Dwight Kuhn**: 46, 55 (Grasshopper) **Maslowski Wildlife Productions**: 39 (Least), 50, 210, 213, 216, 318, 320 (top and bottom insets) **Tom McHugh/PRI***: 56, 65 (Desert), 77 (Sagebrush) **Anthony Mercieca/DPA***: 65 (White-throated) **28 Adam Messer/MFWP***: 49 (Olive-backed) **Gary Meszaros/DPA***: 37 (top), 52 (inset), 104 **Alan Nelson/DPA***: 172 (Northern) **Stan Osolinski/DPA***: 212 **James F. Parnell**: 37 (bottom) **Dusty Perin/DPA***: 160 **B. Moose Peterson/WRP***: 39 (Water), 49 (Great), 77 (Long-tailed), 91 (Long-eared), 110 (middle inset), 114 (main), 142 (main), 162 (both) **Rod Planck**: 202 **Rod Planck/DPA***: 196 (winter), 204 (winter) **Jim Roetzel/DPA***: 246 **Merlin D. Tuttle/BCI***: 88 (main), 90 (Small-footed), 91 (Spotted, Yuma, Allen's) **John and Gloria Tveten**: 49 (Hispid), 52 (main), 54 (Western), 65 (Eastern), 90 (Fringed) **John and Gloria Tveten/KAC***: 39 (Desert, Dwarf), 44, 49 (Silky), 54 (Pinyon), 55 (Plains, Rock, Brush), 71 (both), 77 (Mountain), 116 **Stan Tekiela**: all other photos

*ASM: American Society of Mammalogists; BCI: Bat Conservation International, Inc.; DPA: Dembinsky Photo Associates; KAC: KAC Productions; MFWP: Montana Fish, Wildlife & Parks; PRI: Photo Researchers, Inc.; WRP: Wildlife Research Photography

To the best of the publisher's knowledge, all photos were of live mammals. Some were photographed in a controlled condition.

10 9 8 7 6

Mammals of Colorado Field Guide
Copyright © 2007 by Stan Tekiela
Published by Adventure Publications, an imprint of AdventureKEEN
310 Garfield Street South
Cambridge, Minnesota 55008
(800) 678-7006
www.adventurepublications.net
Printed in China
ISBN 978-1-59193-197-3 (pbk.)

TABLE OF CONTENTS

COLORADO'S MAMMALS

Colorado is a great place for wildlife watchers! This state is one of the few places to see magnificent mammals such as the Bighorn Sheep. We also have a large population of Elk, along with many interesting animals such as the Ringtail and Abert's Squirrel. While Bobcats and fleet-footed Snowshoe Hares make their homes in the coniferous mountain forests of Colorado, the foothills are great places to catch glimpses of Mule Deer and Mountain Cottontails. In eastern parts of the state, there are jackrabbits and prairie dogs that are always fun to watch. No matter where you may be in Colorado, there is a wide variety of mammals to see and enjoy.

WHAT IS A MAMMAL?

The first mammals appeared in the late Triassic Period, about 200 million years ago. These ancient mammals were small, lacked diversity and looked nothing like our current-day mammals. During the following Jurassic Period, mammal size and diversity started to increase. Mammals generally started to appear more like today's mammals in the Cenozoic Era, which occurred after the mass extinction of dinosaurs, about 60 million years ago.

Today, modern mammals are a large group of animals that includes nearly 5,500 species around the world, with more than 400 species in North America. Here in Colorado, we have 130 species. Except for the House Mouse, Norway Rat, Feral Pig and Feral Horse, the mammals of Colorado are native to the state. They range from the tiny Least Shrew, which is no larger than a human thumb, to the extremely large and majestic Moose, which can grow to nearly 8 feet (2.4 m) tall and weigh up to 1,400 pounds (630 kg).

All mammals have some common traits or characteristics. Mammals have a backbone (vertebra) and are warm-blooded (endothermic). In endothermic animals, the process of eating and breaking down food in the digestive tract produces heat, which keeps the animal warm even on cold winter nights. Except during periods of hibernation or torpor, the body temperature of mammals stays within a narrow range, just as it does in people. Body temperature is controlled with rapid, open-mouthed breathing known as panting, by shunting blood flow to or away from areas with networks of blood vessels, such as ears, for cooling or conserving heat. When blood flows through vessels that are close to the surface of skin, heat is released and the body cools. When blood flows away from the surface of skin, heat is conserved.

Most mammals are covered with a thick coat of fur or hair. Fur is critical for survival and needs to be kept clean and in good condition. Very few animals would be able to survive a Colorado winter without the amazing insulating qualities of fur. In some animals, such as the Northern River Otter, the fur is so thick it keeps the underlying skin warm and dry even while swimming. Just as birds must preen their feathers to maintain good health, animals spend hours each day licking and "combing" or grooming their fur. You can easily observe this grooming behavior in your pet cat or dog.

Mammals share several other characteristics. All females bear live young and suckle their babies with milk produced from the mammary glands. Mother's milk provides young mammals with total nourishment during the first part of their lives. Also, mammals have sound-conducting bones in their middle ears. These bones give animals the ability to hear as humans do and, in many cases, hear much better.

Mammals are diphyodont, meaning they have two sets of teeth. There are milk or deciduous teeth, which fall out, and permanent teeth, also known as adult teeth. Adult teeth usually consist of incisors, canines, premolars and molars, but these categories can be highly variable in each mammal family. Teeth are often used to classify or group mammals into families in the same manner as the bill of a bird is used to classify or group birds into families.

Reproduction in mammals can be complex and difficult to understand. Many mammals have delayed implantation, which means after the egg and sperm have joined (impregnation), the resulting embryo remains in a suspended state until becoming implanted in the uterine wall. The delay time can be anywhere from a few days to weeks or months. An animal that becomes stressed from lack of food will pass the embryo out of the reproductive tract, and no pregnancy occurs. Conversely, well-fed mothers may have twins or even triplets. Bats and some other species store sperm in the reproductive tract over winter. Impregnation is delayed until spring, and implantation occurs right after impregnation. This process is known as delayed impregnation.

Most mammals are nocturnal, secretive and don't make a lot of noise, so they tend to go unnoticed. Signs of mammals, such as tracks or scat, are often more commonly seen than the actual animal. However, if you spend some time in the right habitat at the right time of day, your chances of seeing mammals will increase.

IDENTIFICATION STEP-BY-STEP

Fortunately, most large mammals are easy to identify and are not confused with other species. This is not the case, however, with small mammals such as mice or voles. Small animals, while plentiful, can be a challenge to correctly identify because they often have only minor differences in teeth or internal organs and bones.

This field guide is organized by families, starting with small animals, such as shrews and mice, and ending with large mammals such as bear and horse. Within each family section, the animals are in size order from small to large.

Each mammal has four to six pages of color photos and text, with a silhouette of the animal illustrated on the first description page. Each silhouette is located in a quick-compare tab in the upper right corner. Decide which animal group you are seeing, use the quick-compare tabs to locate the pages for that group, then compare the photos with your animal. If you aren't sure of the identity, the text on description pages explains identifying features that may or may not be easily seen. The first description page for each species also has a compare section with notes about similar species in this field guide. Other pertinent details and the naturalist facts in Stan's Notes will help you correctly identify your mammal in question. Photos of other species will help you identify all of the mammals of Colorado.

Thus, every effort has been made to provide relevant identification information including range maps, which can help you eliminate some choices. Colored areas of the maps show where a species can be seen, but not the density of the species. While ranges are accurately depicted, they change on an ongoing basis due to a variety of factors. Please use the maps as intended—as a general guide only.

Finally, if you already know the name of your animal, simply use the index to quickly find the page and learn more about the species from the text and photos.

For many people, an animal's track or silhouette is all they might see of an animal. However, tracks in mud or snow and silhouettes are frequently difficult to identify. Special quick-compare pages, beginning on page 14, are a great place to start the identification process. These pages group similar kinds of animals and tracks side by side for easy comparison. For example, all hoofed animals, such as sheep and bison, are grouped in one section and all dog-like animals are grouped in another. Within the groupings, silhouettes and tracks are illustrated in relative size from small to large. This format allows you to compare one silhouette or track shape and size with another that is similarly shaped and sized. When you don't know whether you're seeing the silhouette or track of a coyote or wolf, a deer or elk or other similar species, use the quick-compare pages for quick and easy reference.

To begin, find the group that your unknown silhouette or track looks similar to and start comparing. Since each group has relatively few animals, it won't take long to narrow your choices. A ruler can be handy to measure your track and compare it with the size given in the book. To confirm the identity of the silhouette or track and for more detailed information about the animal, refer to the description pages for the number of toes, length of stride and other distinguishing characteristics.

TAXONOMY OF COLORADO'S MAMMALS

Biologists classify mammals based on their ancestry and physical characteristics. Colorado's mammals are grouped into nine scientific orders. Charts with the scientific classification (taxonomy) are shown on the Appendix, pages 356-367. Each of the nine charts starts with one of the orders and shows all of the scientific families and mammals in that particular order.

CAUTION

Hunting, trapping, possessing and other activities involving animals are regulated by the Colorado Department of Natural Resources (DNR), Colorado Division of Wildlife (DOW). You should familiarize yourself with the laws and seasons before doing any kill trapping, live trapping and hunting.

As interesting as all of these animals are, resist any temptation to capture any animal for a pet. Wild animals, even babies, never make good pets. Wild animals often have specific dietary and habitat requirements that rarely can be duplicated in a captive situation, and many will not survive. In many cases, capturing animals for pets is also illegal. This practice not only diminishes the population, it reduces the possibility for future reproduction. Furthermore, some animals are uncommon in Colorado, and their populations can be even more quickly depleted.

Live trapping of animals in an attempt to rid your yard of them rarely works. The removal of an animal from its habitat creates a void that is quickly filled with a neighboring animal or its offspring, recreating the original situation. Moreover, an unfortunate animal that is live trapped and moved to a new location often cannot find a habitat with an adequate food supply, shelter or a territory that is not already occupied. Animals that have been moved often die from exposure to weather, are struck by vehicles while crossing roads or killed by resident animals. With habitat ranges growing smaller every year, removing just one animal can have a direct impact on the local population of a species. We can all learn to live with our wild animals with just a few modifications to our yards and attitudes. Observe and record animals with your camera, but leave them where they belong—in the wild.

Encounters with wildlife often involve injured or orphaned animals. Many well-intentioned people with little or no resources or knowledge of what is needed try to care for such animals. Injured or orphaned animals deserve the best care, so please do the right thing if you find one and turn it over to a licensed professional wildlife rehabilitator. Information about wildlife rehabilitation in Colorado is listed in the resource section of this field guide. The rehabilitation staff may often be able to give you updates on the condition of an animal you bring in and even when it is released. When you take an animal to a rehab center, you might also want to consider making a monetary donation to help cover the costs involved for its care.

Enjoy the Mammals!

Stan

Body length measurements
do not include tail.

Average size of the smallest and
largest of this group compared to
an 8" hand.

Silhouettes are in proportion by
average body length. Tracks are in
proportion by average largest
foot. Front track is on the left and
hind is on the right.

1⅞"
Least Shrew
pg. 39

⅛" ⅜"

2"
Masked Shrew
pg. 35

⅛" ⅜"

3¼"
House Mouse
pg. 54

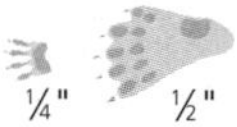

¼" ½"

3⅜"
Dwarf Shrew
pg. 39

¼" ⅜"

3⅝"
**White-footed
Mouse** pg. 49

¼" ¾"

3¾"
Deer Mouse
pg. 51

¼" ¾"

3¾"
Merriam's Shrew
pg. 39

⅜" ½"

3⅞"
Canyon Mouse
pg. 55

¾" 1"

4"
**Northern Grasshopper
Mouse** pg. 55

½" 1"

4¼"
Montane Shrew
pg. 39

⅜" ½"

14

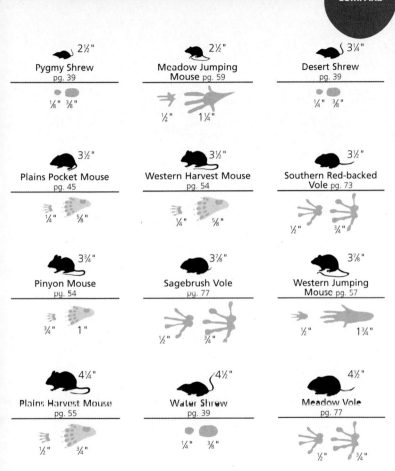

Pygmy Shrew pg. 39 — 2½"
⅛" ⅜"

Meadow Jumping Mouse pg. 59 — 2½"
½" 1¼"

Desert Shrew pg. 39 — 3¼"
¼" ⅜"

Plains Pocket Mouse pg. 45 — 3½"
¼" ⅝"

Western Harvest Mouse pg. 54 — 3½"
¼" ⅝"

Southern Red-backed Vole pg. 73 — 3½"
½" ¾"

Pinyon Mouse pg. 54 — 3¾"
¾" 1"

Sagebrush Vole pg. 77 — 3⅞"
½" ¾"

Western Jumping Mouse pg. 57 — 3⅞"
½" 1¾"

Plains Harvest Mouse pg. 55 — 4¼"
½" ¾"

Water Shrew pg. 39 — 4½"
¼" ⅜"

Meadow Vole pg. 77 — 4½"
½" ¾"

Similar species on next page 15

Body length measurements do not include tail.

Average size of the smallest and largest of this group compared to an 8" hand.

Silhouettes are in proportion by average body length. Tracks are in proportion by average largest foot. Front track is on the left and hind is on the right.

4½"
Prairie Vole
pg. 77

½"   ⅞"

4⅝"
Mexican Vole
pg. 77

½"   ¾"

4⅞"
Heather Vole
pg. 77

½"   ¾"

4⅞"
Montane Vole
pg. 77

¾"   1"

5¼"
Olive-backed Pocket Mouse pg. 49

½"   ¾"

5½"
Eastern Mole
pg. 41

1½"   ⅝"

6½"
Desert Woodrat
pg. 65

⅞"   1⅜"

8⅞"
White-throated Woodrat pg. 65

1"   1½"

9"
Mexican Woodrat
pg. 65

1"   1½"

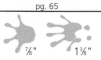
9"
Norway Rat
pg. 67

1"   1½"

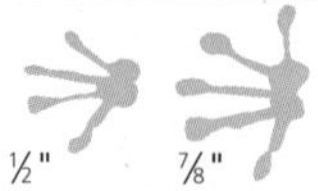

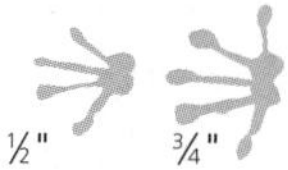

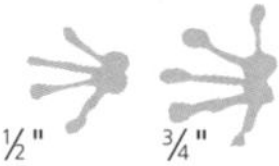

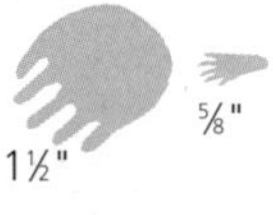

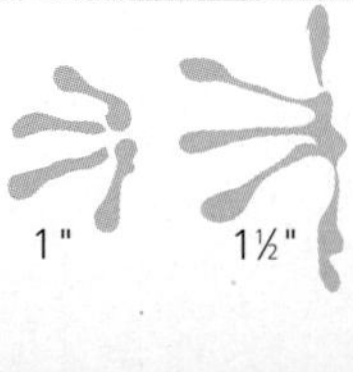

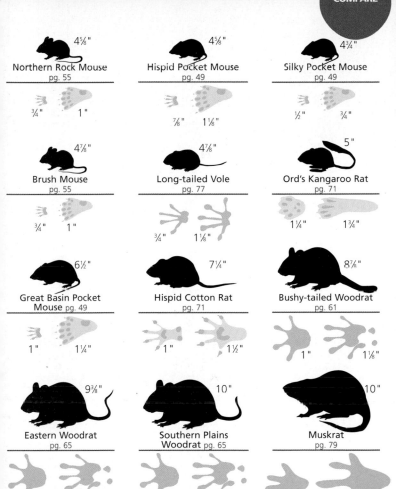

4⅝"
Northern Rock Mouse
pg. 55
¾"   1"

4⅝"
Hispid Pocket Mouse
pg. 49
⅞"   1⅛"

4¾"
Silky Pocket Mouse
pg. 49
½"   ¾"

4⅞"
Brush Mouse
pg. 55
¾"   1"

4⅞"
Long-tailed Vole
pg. 77
¾"   1⅛"

5"
Ord's Kangaroo Rat
pg. 71
1¼"   1¾"

6½"
Great Basin Pocket Mouse pg. 49
1"   1¼"

7¼"
Hispid Cotton Rat
pg. 71
1"   1½"

8⅞"
Bushy-tailed Woodrat
pg. 61
1"   1⅛"

9⅜"
Eastern Woodrat
pg. 65
1¼"   1¾"

10"
Southern Plains Woodrat pg. 65
1¼"   1¾"

10"
Muskrat
pg. 79
1½"   3"

17

Body length measurements do not include tail.

Average size of the smallest and largest of this group compared to an 8" hand.

Silhouettes are in proportion to each other by average body length.

1¾"

Little Brown Bat
pg. 90

no tracks

2¼"

Western Small-footed Myotis pg. 90

no tracks

2½"

Big Brown Bat
pg. 87

no tracks

2½"

Red Bat
pg. 90

no tracks

2¾"

Spotted Bat
pg. 91

no tracks

2¾"

Yuma Myotis
pg. 91

no tracks

3¼"

Long-legged Myotis
pg. 91

no tracks

3¾"

Cave Myotis
pg. 91

no tracks

Fringed Myotis
pg. 90
no tracks

Western Pipistrelle
pg. 90
no tracks

Brazilian Free-tailed Bat
pg. 90
no tracks

Silver-haired Bat
pg. 91
no tracks

California Myotis
pg. 91
no tracks

Townsend's Big-eared Bat pg. 91
no tracks

Long-eared Myotis
pg. 91
no tracks

Allen's Big-eared Bat
pg. 91
no tracks

Hoary Bat
pg. 91
no tracks

Big Free-tailed Bat
pg. 91
no tracks

Body length measurements do not include tail.

Average size of the smallest and largest of this group compared to a 6' human.

Silhouettes are in proportion by average body length. Tracks are in proportion by average largest foot. Front track is on the left and hind is on the right.

 3½"

Least Chipmunk
pg. 93

½"   1 "

 3⅝"

Hopi Chipmunk
pg. 97

⅝"   1¼"

 6"

Botta's Pocket Gopher
pg. 177

⅞"   ¾"

 6½"

White-tailed Antelope Squirrel pg. 113

¾"   1½"

 8"

Northern Flying Squirrel
pg. 141

¾"   1½"

 8"

Pine Squirrel
pg. 145

¾"   1½"

 8¼"

Golden-mantled Ground Squirrel pg. 125

¾"   1½"

 9½"

Wyoming Ground Squirrel pg. 133

¾"   1½"

 10"

Abert's Squirrel
pg. 149

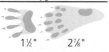
1½"   2⅞"

 11¼"

Gunnison's Prairie Dog pg. 157

1"   2¼"

20

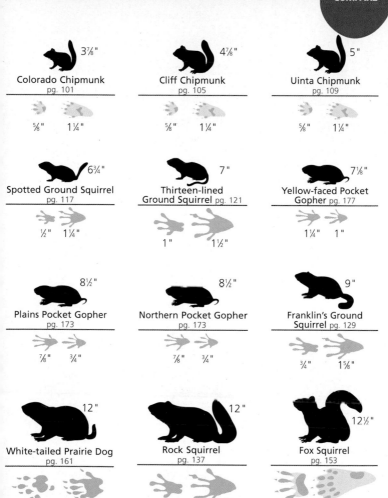

3⅞"
Colorado Chipmunk
pg. 101
⅝"   1¼"

4⅞"
Cliff Chipmunk
pg. 105
⅝"   1¼"

5"
Uinta Chipmunk
pg. 109
⅝"   1¼"

6¾"
Spotted Ground Squirrel
pg. 117
½"   1¼"

7"
Thirteen-lined
Ground Squirrel pg. 121
1"   1½"

7⅛"
Yellow-faced Pocket
Gopher pg. 177
1¼"   1"

8½"
Plains Pocket Gopher
pg. 173
⅞"   ¾"

8½"
Northern Pocket Gopher
pg. 173
⅞"   ¾"

9"
Franklin's Ground
Squirrel pg. 129
¾"   1⅝"

12"
White-tailed Prairie Dog
pg. 161
1"   2¼"

12"
Rock Squirrel
pg. 137
1½"   2¼"

12½"
Fox Squirrel
pg. 153
1½"   2⅞"

Similar species on next page   21

Body length measurements
do not include tail.

Average size of the smallest and
largest of this group compared to
a 6' human.

13"

Black-tailed Prairie Dog
pg. 165

1"   2¼"

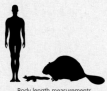

Body length measurements
do not include tail.

Average size of the smallest and
largest of this group compared to
a 6' human.

13¾"

Ringtail
pg. 247

1¾"   2⅝"

18"

Nine-banded Armadillo
pg. 255

1⅝"   2"

27½"

Virginia Opossum
pg. 263

1½"   2"

Silhouettes are in proportion by
average body length. Tracks are in
proportion by average largest
foot. Front track is on the left and
hind is on the right.

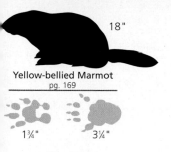

18"

Yellow-bellied Marmot
pg. 169

1¾" 3¼"

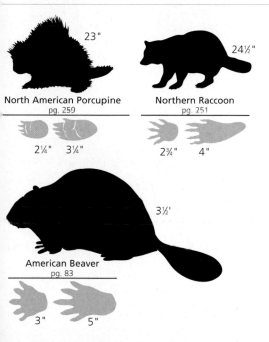

23"

North American Porcupine
pg. 259

2¼" 3¼"

24½"

Northern Raccoon
pg. 251

2¾" 4"

3½'

American Beaver
pg. 83

3" 5"

Body length measurements
do not include tail.

Average size of the smallest and
largest of this group compared to
a 6' human.

Silhouettes are in proportion by
average body length. Tracks are in
proportion by average largest
foot. Front track is on the left and
hind is on the right.

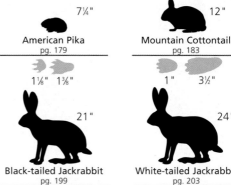

7¼"

American Pika
pg. 179

1⅛" 1⅜"

12"

Mountain Cottontail
pg. 183

1" 3½"

21"

Black-tailed Jackrabbit
pg. 199

1" 4¾"

24"

White-tailed Jackrabbit
pg. 203

1" 5½"

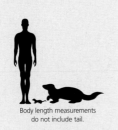

Body length measurements
do not include tail.

Average size of the smallest and
largest of this group compared to
a 6' human.

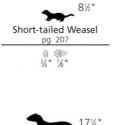

8½"

Short-tailed Weasel
pg. 207

¾" ⅞"

10¾"

Western Spotted Skunk
pg. 239

1" 1½"

17¼"

Black-footed Ferret
pg. 223

2¼" 2⅜"

22"

Striped Skunk
pg. 243

1⅜" 2¾"

12¾"
Desert Cottontail
pg. 187

1"   3½"

 16"
Eastern Cottontail
pg. 191

1"   3½"

 17½"
Snowshoe Hare
pg. 195

1"   4½"

 12"
Long-tailed Weasel
pg. 211

¾" ⅞"

 16½"
American Marten
pg. 215

1½"   1⅝"

 17"
Mink
pg. 219

1½"   2⅝"

 25"
American Badger
pg. 227

2"   2"

 30½"
Wolverine
pg. 231

5"   5"

 36"
Northern River Otter
pg. 235

3⅜"   3½"

25

Body length measurements
do not include tail.

Average size of the smallest and largest of this group compared to a 6' human.

Body length measurements
do not include tail.

Average size of the smallest and largest of this group compared to a 6' human.

Silhouettes are in proportion by average body length. Tracks are in proportion by average largest foot. Front track is on the left and hind is on the right.

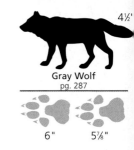

18"

Kit Fox
pg. 267

1½" 1⅜"

18"

Swift Fox
pg. 271

1½" 1⅜"

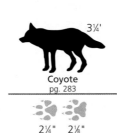

3¼'

Coyote
pg. 283

2¼" 2⅛"

4½'

Gray Wolf
pg. 287

6" 5⅞"

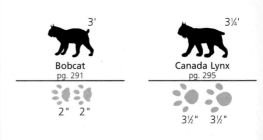

3'

Bobcat
pg. 291

2" 2"

3¼'

Canada Lynx
pg. 295

3½" 3½"

26

Gray Fox
pg. 275

1½" 1¾"

Red Fox
pg. 279

2"   1⅞"

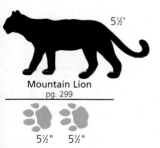

Mountain Lion
pg. 299

5½"   5½"

Body length measurements
do not include tail.

Average size of the smallest and largest of this group compared to a 6' human.

Body length measurements
do not include tail.

Average size of the smallest and largest of this group compared to a 6' human.

Silhouettes are in proportion by average body length. Tracks are in proportion by average largest foot. Front track is on the left and hind is on the right.

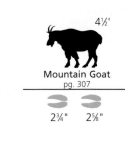

4¼'

Pronghorn
pg. 303

3"   2⅞"

4½'

Mountain Goat
pg. 307

2¾"   2⅝"

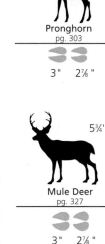

5¾'

Mule Deer
pg. 327

3"   2⅞"

6'

Feral Horse
pg. 347

4"   4"

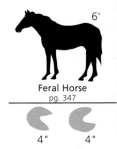

5¼'

Black Bear
pg. 339

4"   8"

6½'

Grizzly Bear
pg. 343

6½"   12"

5'

Bighorn Sheep
pg. 311

2¾"   2⅝"

5'

Feral Pig
pg. 319

2¾"   2⅝"

5½'

White-tailed Deer
pg. 323

2¾"   2⅝"

8'

Moose
pg. 331

5½"   5⅜"

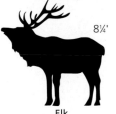

8¼'

Elk
pg. 335

4¼"   4⅛"

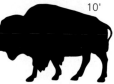

10'

American Bison
pg. 315

6½"   6⅜"

29

Common Name

Range Map *Scientific name* Shape

Family: common family name (scientific family name)

Size: (L) average length or range of length of body from head to rump; (T) average length or range of length of tail; (H) average height or range of height to top of back

Weight: average weight or range of weight, may include (M) male and (F) female weights

Description: brief description of the mammal, may include color morphs, seasonal variations or differences between male and female

Origin/Age: native or non-native to Colorado; average life span in the wild

Compare: notes about other species that look similar and the pages on which they can be found, may include extra information to help identify

Habitat: environment where the animal is found (e.g., forests, prairies, wetlands)

Home: description of nest, burrow or den; may include other related information

Food: herbivore, carnivore, insectivore, omnivore; what the animal eats most of the time; may include other related information

Sounds: vocalization or other noises the animal creates; may include variant sounds or other information

Breeding: mating season; length of gestation; may include additional comments

Young: number of offspring born per year and when; may include description or birth weight

31

summer coat

winter coat

silver morph   black morph

sample page

Signs: evidence that the animal was there or is near; may include a description of scat; other comments

Activity: diurnal, nocturnal, crepuscular; other comments

scat

Tracks: forepaw and hind paw or hoof size and shape, largest size first; pattern of tracks; description of prints, may include stride; other comments

Tracks and Pattern

Stan's Notes: Interesting gee-whiz natural history information. This can be something to look or listen for, or something to help positively identify the animal such as remarkable features. May include additional photos to illustrate juveniles, nests, unique behaviors and other key characteristics.

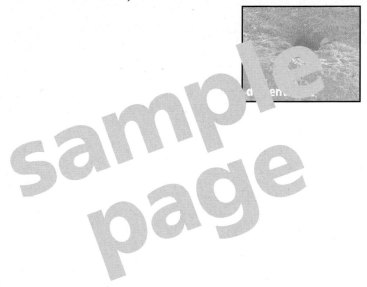

kits

Masked Shrew

Sorex cinereus

Family: Shrews (Soricidae)

Size: L 1¾-2¼" (4.5-5.5 cm); T 1-2" (2.5-5 cm)

Weight: ¼ oz. (7 g)

Description: Overall brown to gray with lighter gray-to-white belly. A very long, pointed snout. Tiny dark eyes. Ears slightly visible. Long hairy tail, brown above and lighter below with a dark tuft at tip.

Origin/Age: native; 1-2 years

Compare: The small size, brown color and long tail of the Masked Shrew help distinguish it from the other shrews in Colorado. The Pygmy Shrew (pg. 39) is slightly larger.

Habitat: mountain meadows, subalpine forests, willow thickets, elevations from 5,000-11,000' (1,525-3,355 m)

Home: nest, 4-6" (10-15 cm) wide, made of leaves and grasses, under a log or rock

Food: insectivore, carnivore; insects, ants, slugs, spiders, earthworms, small mammals such as mice

Sounds: inconsequential; sharp squeaks and high-pitched whistles

Breeding: spring to autumn mating; 18 days gestation

Young: 5-7 offspring 2-3 times per year; young are born naked with eyes closed, eyes open at 17-19 days, weaned at about 20 days, on own within days of being weaned, young born in fall are less likely to survive due to lack of food

Signs: tiny tunnels or runways in freshly dug soil; shrew is rarely, if ever, seen

Activity: diurnal, nocturnal; active under snow in winter

Tracks: hind paw ¼-½" (.6-1 cm) long, forepaw slightly smaller; 1 set of 4 tracks, but prints are so close together they appear as 1 track; 4 prints together are 1" square (6.4 sq. cm), sometimes has a slight tail drag mark

Stan's Notes: This very secretive, solitary animal is rarely seen because of its underground lifestyle. Also called Cinereus Shrew, it is one of the smallest mammals in Colorado. It is also one of the most widespread mammals in North America, ranging all across Canada and Alaska and the northern-tiered states.

Its long pointed snout is characteristic of all 33 species of shrews seen in North America. Gives off a strong musky odor, which makes it unattractive to large mammalian predators, but the scent does not seem to deter birds of prey such as owls and hawks. Heart rate will race to as many as 1,200 beats per minute when it is excited. Can die from fright when captured.

Has little body mass due to its small size, so it must feed nearly every hour to keep warm or starve to death. Moves constantly, darting about to find food. Often eats more than its own body weight daily in worms, slugs and beetles. Will kill mice, which are larger than itself. Seeks dormant insects and larvae in winter. Does not hibernate.

A desirable animal to have around your home and yard because it eats many harmful insects and keeps populations of mice in check. Does not transmit rabies and is not harmful to humans.

Similar species on next page

All shrews in Colorado are insect-eating small mammals. Ranging in color from gray to brown and black, they appear similar to mice, but shrews have longer, more pointed snouts and well-haired tails.

Shrews live in the shallow tunnels of other small mammals such as voles and moles. They have extremely high metabolic rates, so they forage for food round-the-clock, consuming their own body weight in food every 24 hours. All shrew species have poor eyesight, but they have an excellent sense of smell and the ability to hear in very high frequencies. Some are thought to sense electromagnetic fields, enabling them to find prey in complete darkness.

Least Shrew 1½-2¼"

Pygmy Shrew 2-3"

Desert Shrew 3-3½"

Dwarf Shrew 3-3¾"

Water Shrew 4-5"

Not pictured:
Merriam's Shrew 3-4½"
Montane Shrew 4-4½"

Eastern Mole

Scalopus aquaticus

Family: Moles (Talpidae)

Size: L 4-7" (10-18 cm); T ¾-1¼" (2-3 cm)

Weight: 3-5 oz. (85-142 g)

Description: Short silky fur, dark brown to gray with a silver sheen. Long pointed snout. Very large, naked front feet, more wide than long and resembling human hands with palms turned outward. Very short, nearly naked tail. Pinpoint eyes, frequently hidden by fur. Male slightly larger than female.

Origin/Age: native; 1-2 years

Compare: Very unique-looking animal with extremely short legs and large, human-like pink hands for paws. No eyes and a short tail. Smaller than the pocket gophers (pp. 173-177), all of which have eyes and longer tails.

Habitat: dry grassy areas, fields, lawns, gardens, loose well-drained soils

Home: burrow, tunnels usually are 4-20" (10-50 cm) underground in summer, deeper tunnels below the frost line during winter, nest is in a chamber connected to a tunnel, with separate chambers for giving birth and raising young

Food: insectivore, herbivore; insects, grubs, roots, earthworms

Sounds: inconsequential; rarely, if ever, heard

Breeding: Feb-Mar mating; 32-42 days gestation

Young: 2-6 offspring once per year in early spring; born naked with eyes closed, weaned at 30-40 days, leaves nest chamber when weaned

41

Signs: ridges of soil from tunnel construction just below the surface of the ground, sometimes small piles of soil on the ground (molehills) from digging deeper permanent tunnels

Activity: diurnal, nocturnal; active year-round, does not appear to time its activities with the rising and setting of the sun

Tracks: hind paw ⅝" (1.5 cm) long with 5 toes, forepaw 1½" (4 cm) long with 5 toes; individual tracks are indistinguishable and create a single groove with claw marks, sometimes has a tail drag mark; spends almost all of its time in its underground tunnel system, so tracks are rarely seen

Stan's Notes: The first time this animal was described in records was when a drowned mole was found in a well. It was presumed, in error, to be aquatic; hence the Latin species name *aquaticus,* which also refers to the slight webbing between its toes. This is the most subterranean mammal in Colorado, spending 99 percent of its life underground. Also called Common Mole or just Mole.

The Eastern Mole has no external ears. Its tiny eyes are covered with skin and detect light only, not shapes or colors. It has large white teeth, unlike the shrews, which have chestnut or tan teeth. Uses its very sensitive, flexible snout to find food by smelling and sensing vibrations with its whiskers. The nap of its short fur can lie forward or backward, making it easier to travel in either direction in tight tunnels. A narrow pelvis allows it to somersault often and reverse its heading.

Excavates its own tunnel system. Uses its front feet to dig while pushing loosened soil back and out of the way with its hind feet. Able to dig 1 foot (30 cm) per minute in loose soil. Digging and tunneling is beneficial to the environment; it aerates the soil and allows moisture to penetrate deeper into the ground.

Searches for subterranean insects, earthworms, some plant roots and other food in temporary tunnels, usually located just below the surface of the ground. Deeper permanent tunnels are used for living, nesting and depositing waste. Will move to even deeper tunnels below the frost line during winter.

The male will seek out a female in her tunnel to mate during late winter. It is thought that a female rarely leaves her tunnel system, except when a young female leaves the tunnels of her mother to establish her own.

Unlike most other small mammals, it reproduces only once each year. Not preyed upon as heavily due to its burrowing (fossorial) life, so does not need to reproduce often.

Plains Pocket Mouse
Perognathus flavescens

Family: Kangaroo Rats and Pocket Mice
(Heteromyidae)

Size: L 3-4" (7.5-10 cm); T 1¾-2¼" (4.5-5.5 cm)

Weight: ¼-½ oz. (7-14 g)

Description: Overall tan to yellowish brown or reddish brown with a wash of black hairs concentrated near the center of the back. White chest, belly, legs and feet. Bicolored tail, dark above and white below. Large eyes. Small round ears, often with a white patch just beneath each ear.

Origin/Age: native; 1-2 years

Compare: Other species of pocket mice (pp. 48-49) in the state are very similar in size and color. The Olive-backed Pocket Mouse (pg. 49) is more olive in color and has a yellowish stripe on its sides.

Habitat: sagebrush, prairies, coniferous forests, unmowed grassy areas along fences (fencerows), ditches, farm fields, elevations below 6,000' (1,830 m)

Home: nest made of dried plant material, in an underground burrow

Food: omnivore; seeds, vegetation, fruit, nuts, insects, earthworms

Sounds: inconsequential; scratching or scampering can be heard

Breeding: May-Jul mating; 20-23 days gestation

Young: 3-4 pups up to 2 times per year; born naked and deaf with eyes closed, juvenile is gray with a white belly

45

Signs: evidence of a burrow under clumps of vegetation, runways and surface tunnels radiating from the entrance of burrow; scat not seen

Activity: nocturnal, crepuscular; remains in the nest during the coldest winter days or during heavy rain in summer

Tracks: hind paw ½-¾" (1-2 cm) long with 5 toes, forepaw ¼" (.6 cm) long with 4 toes; 1 set of 4 tracks

Stan's Notes: This is a species that can have highly variable color, often matching the color of the soil in which it lives. It is the most common species in grasslands with sandy soils in Colorado.

Feeds mainly on seeds. Will gather larger seeds, storing them in its underground burrow to eat later. Also consumes insects when they are available.

Digs shallow burrows with several chambers only a few inches deep, with several entrances. Plugs the entrance holes to burrow in safety during the day.

Usually active aboveground in Colorado only from March through October. Not a true hibernator. Thought to enter a state of deep sleep known as torpor during cold spells in winter.

Home ranges are very small, with most adults spending their entire life in an area less than 20 feet (6.1 m) wide. Males have a slightly larger territory than females.

Similar species on next page

Despite the common name "Mouse," pocket mice are not a type of mouse, nor are they closely related to any other mammal species in North America. Pocket mice are found only west of the Mississippi River, where they are mainly seen in open fields, prairies and deserts. They live underground in burrows and prefer sandy soils, which allow them to dig more easily into the earth.

All pocket mice are nocturnal. They have coarse fur, often with stiff bristles, and fur-lined cheek pouches in which to carry food and nesting material. Unlike jumping mice, pocket mice are not good jumpers.

Hispid Pocket Mouse 4¼-5"

Silky Pocket Mouse 4½-5"

Olive-backed Pocket Mouse 5-5½"

Great Basin Pocket Mouse 5½-7½"

Deer Mouse
Peromyscus maniculatus

Family: Rats and Mice (Muridae)

Size: L 3-4½" (7.5-11 cm); T 2-4" (5-10 cm)

Weight: ⅜-1¼ oz. (11-35 g)

Description: Back and sides highly variable in color from gray to reddish brown. Chest, belly, legs and feet are always white. Sharply bicolored tail, dark above and white below, as long as head and body. Large bulging eyes. Large round ears.

Origin/Age: native; 1-2 years

Compare: The tail of the Deer Mouse is slightly longer than that of White-footed Mouse (pg. 54). However, it is extremely difficult to differentiate these species because of their remarkable similarities. The Deer Mouse is the most common mouse species in the entire state.

Habitat: nearly all habitats including woodlands, prairies, mountains, fields, wetlands and areas around dwellings, all elevations

Home: nest made of dried plant material and moss, in a small depression in the ground or in an above-ground cavity

Food: omnivore; seeds, vegetation, fruit, nuts, insects, earthworms, baby birds, baby mice, carrion

Sounds: inconsequential; scratching or scampering can be heard, drums front feet on ground if threatened

Breeding: Mar-Oct mating; 21-25 days gestation

Young: 1-8 (average 5) pups up to 3 times per year; born naked and deaf with eyes closed, juvenile is gray with a white belly, leaves mother at 3 weeks

51

Signs: strong smell of urine in the areas it often visits, including its large nest made from dried plant material; small, hard black droppings the size of a pinhead

Activity: nocturnal, crepuscular; active year-round, stays in nest during the coldest winter days or during heavy rain in summer

Tracks: hind paw ¾" (2 cm) long with 5 toes, forepaw ¼" (.6 cm) long with 4 toes; 1 set of 4 tracks; sometimes has a tail drag mark, often a short single groove on the surface of snow between ridges of snow made by tunneling

Stan's Notes: The most common mouse in Colorado and the most widespread rodent in North America. Found in just about every habitat from the Arctic Circle to the rain forests in Central America. More than 100 subspecies have been described with several occurring in Colorado; differences are in tail length and ear size. Deer Mice look different in different parts of the world (morphologically variable), more so than other mice species.

An important food source for other animals such as foxes, hawks, coyotes and owls. Lives mostly on the ground. Tunnels beneath snow to the surface of the ground and also runs around on top of snow. May have several emergency escape tunnels in addition to the tunnel that leads to its nest.

Very tame and not aggressive. Climbs trees and shrubs to reach seeds and leaves. Caches food for winter, storing seeds and small nuts in protected areas outside the nest.

Builds nest during late fall or early winter in a bluebird nest box or in another birdhouse if the box is not left open for the winter. Usually solitary, but will gather in small groups in winter, usually females with young, to huddle and conserve heat. However, their combined urine quickly soaks nesting material, necessitating a move to another nest box or natural cavity. Readily enters homes looking for shelter and food.

Sexually mature at 5-7 weeks. Male may stay with female briefly after mating, but frequently lives a solitary life. Female is more territorial than the male, but male has a larger home range. Home territory ranges from a few hundred square feet to a couple acres.

A primary host for the virulent hantavirus that causes Hantaviral Pulmonary Syndrome (HPS), a serious disease in humans. Great care must be taken not to breathe in dust or other debris when cleaning out a birdhouse with a Deer Mouse nest.

Similar species on next page

To many people, all mice look the same. There are many common features among species that make differentiation very difficult. To make things worse, some species hybridize, creating varieties that defy identification. While some species, such as the House Mouse, can be best identified by where they are found, firm identification of mice should be left to the experts.

House Mouse 2½-4"

Western Harvest Mouse 3-4"

White-footed Mouse 3-4¼"

Pinyon Mouse 3½-4"

Northern Grasshopper Mouse 3-5"

Plains Harvest Mouse 4-4½"

Northern Rock Mouse 4-5¼"

Brush Mouse 4¼-5½"

Not pictured: Canyon Mouse 3½-4¼"

Western Jumping Mouse
Zapus princeps

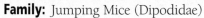

Family: Jumping Mice (Dipodidae)

Size: L 3-4¾" (7.5-12 cm); T 5-6¾" (13-17 cm)

Weight: ¾-1 oz. (21-28 g)

Description: Dark brown down the middle of back. Yellowish brown sides. White-to-yellow belly hair. Large round ears. Prominent dark eyes. Long snout. Extremely long tail, dark above and white below. Very large hind feet.

Origin/Age: native; 1-2 years

Compare: The Meadow Jumping Mouse (pg. 59) is slightly smaller and seen only in north central Colorado, while Western Jumping Mouse is found along streams and in other wet areas in the western half of the state. Other mouse species have shorter tails and belly hair that is gray at the base.

Habitat: along the sides of streams, willow thickets, bogs, marshes, elevations from 6,000-11,500' (1,830-3,510 m)

Home: nest made from dried grass, under a fallen log or clump of grass; used for hibernation

Food: herbivore, insectivore; underground fungi, seeds, fruit, insects

Sounds: inconsequential; scratching or scampering can be heard, drums front feet on ground if threatened

Breeding: May-Jul mating; 17-21 days gestation; will mate shortly after emerging from hibernation

Young: 4-7 pups 2 or more times per year; born naked with eyes closed

57

Signs: surface runways leading in many directions, grasses with missing seed heads (topped), piles of grass stems that are the same length and have seed heads removed

Activity: nocturnal; active 5-6 months of the year, hibernating from October to April or May

Tracks: hind paw 1¾" (4.5 cm) long with a long narrow heel and 5 toes, forepaw ½" (1 cm) long with 4 toes; 1 set of 4 tracks; tracks with tail drag mark seen only in mud during months of activity

Stan's Notes: The jumping mouse got its name from its ability to leap up to 3 feet (1 m) to escape predators or when it is startled. Although the name implies that it jumps to get around, it usually walks on all four feet or moves in a series of small jumps.

Often will remain motionless after jumping several times. Uses its long tail, which is more than 50 percent of its total length, for balance while jumping. Hind legs are longer than front legs and are very fragile, often breaking when live-trapped for research.

Feeds in summer on *Endogone*, an underground fungus that it finds by smell. Does not store food for winter, feeding heavily instead during the last month before it hibernates. Gains up to 100 percent of its body weight in fat. A true hibernator, inactive in winter. Male emerges from hibernation in April, female two weeks later. Some studies show that many may not survive the winter, as only half the population appears the next spring.

Matures sexually before 1 year of age. Many females born in spring are breeding in July. Adults reproduce two times or more each year.

Doesn't cause crop damage. Will rarely enter a dwelling. Jumping mice (genera *Zapus* and *Napaeozapus*) are only in North America.

Additional Jumping Mouse Species

There are just two jumping mouse species in Colorado. The Meadow Jumping Mouse is seen only in a small pocket in north central Colorado. With less than 50 specimens collected in the state, not much is known about the species. Increased expansion of humans has undoubtedly reduced the population.

Meadow Jumping Mouse 2-3"

Bushy-tailed Woodrat
Neotoma cinerea

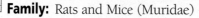

Family: Rats and Mice (Muridae)

Size: L 8-9¾" (20-24.5 cm); T 4-9" (10-22.5 cm)

Weight: 13-15 oz. (369-425 g)

Description: Overall brown with prominent black hairs. Gray-to-white belly, legs and feet. Short stout snout. Large round ears. Dark eyes. Large fuzzy tail, much like a squirrel, flattened lengthwise, gray above and nearly white below.

Origin/Age: native; 4-5 years

Compare: Slightly larger than all other woodrats (pp. 64-65). Look for the squirrel-like furry tail to help identify the Bushy-tailed Woodrat.

Habitat: rocky talus slopes, coniferous forests, old mines, canyons, semideserts, rocky outcrops, elevations up to 10,000' (3,050 m)

Home: nest made with sticks, branches and bones, cup-shaped interior lined with dried grass and other fine plant materials, often constructed at the base of a large tree or up as high as 50' (15 m), also in a shelter such as a cave entrance, under a fallen log or inside an abandoned building

Food: herbivore; wide variety of plants, coniferous seeds and needles, berries, fungi

Sounds: thumping sound created by hind foot drumming

Breeding: Apr-Aug; 20-30 days gestation

Young: 1-6 (average 6) offspring up to 2 times per year; born naked with eyes closed

Signs: large stick house, reminiscent of a bird's nest, containing shiny metal objects; piles of scat, appearing black and tar-like, often in a conspicuous place such as on prominent rocks

Activity: nocturnal; active year-round, can be active on cloudy days

Tracks: hind paw 1-1¼" (2.5-3 cm) long with a wide heel and 5 toes, forepaw 1" (2.5 cm) long with 4 well-spread toes; frequently follows the same paths over and over, making individual tracks difficult to distinguish

Stan's Notes: The Bushy-tailed Woodrat is the most widespread of all woodrat species occurring across the mountainous West, Pacific Northwest and into Canada. Sometimes called Mountain Pack Rat because of the geographic areas it inhabits and the fact that it collects shiny metal or mineral objects. This woodrat is the original pack rat. Under controlled conditions, it will drop the food it is carrying to pick up a shiny coin or other metal object.

Feeds on a wide variety of foods including coniferous tree leaves, seeds, grass, berries and mushrooms. Constructs a stick nest in abandoned buildings or mountain cabins that are not frequently used. Will construct a nest just for food storage and use a second nest for sleeping.

It is reported that most buildings in the mountains have a black tar-like varnish stain from years of woodrat urination and fecal deposits in established "toilets." These toilets are very odoriferous. Once you become familiar with the smell, it is easy to quickly determine the presence of this animal.

Similar species on next page 63

All other species of woodrats in Colorado lack the fuzzy tail of the Bushy-tailed and are much more restricted in their range. The Eastern Woodrat inhabits most of the eastern United States, reaching only into the eastern edge of Colorado. The Mexican Woodrat occurs to the south and is found just in the southern half of Colorado. The same can be said for the White-throated Woodrat, which is seen only in the southern quarter of the state. The Southern Plains Woodrat occurs only in the far southeastern corner of Colorado. The Desert Woodrat is very rare in the state, found only along Colorado's far western edge.

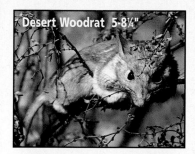

Desert Woodrat 5-8¼"

White-throated Woodrat 8¼-9½"

Mexican Woodrat 8-10"

Eastern Woodrat 7¼-11½"

Southern Plains Woodrat 9¾-10½"

Norway Rat
Rattus norvegicus

Family: Rats and Mice (Muridae)

Size: L 8-10" (20-25 cm); T 5-8" (13-20 cm)

Weight: ½-1 lb. (.2-.5 kg)

Description: Brown to grayish brown above and gray below. Long narrow snout. Large round ears. Dark eyes. Scaly tail, shorter than the body length.

Origin/Age: non-native; 2-4 years

Compare: Larger than all species of mice, voles and shrews. Look for large ears, a long naked tail and narrow pointed snout to help identify. Smaller than the Muskrat (pg. 79), which is rarely seen away from water and never enters homes, barns and other buildings where Norway Rat is typically seen.

Habitat: almost always associated with people in places such as cities, dumps, homes and farms

Home: network of interconnecting tunnels, 2-3" (5-7.5 cm) wide and up to 6' (1.8 m) long, leading to inner chambers used for sleeping and feeding, often has several escape exits and dead-end tunnels for hiding

Food: omnivore; seeds, nuts, insects, carrion, birds, bird eggs, small mammals

Sounds: high-pitched squeaks when squabbling with other rats, scratching or scampering can be heard

Breeding: year-round mating; 20-25 days gestation; female can mate within hours of giving birth

Young: 2-9 (average 6) offspring up to 10 times per year; born naked with eyes closed, eyes open at about 2 weeks, weaned at 3-4 weeks

Signs: holes chewed in barn walls or doors, well-worn paths along walls or that lead in and out of chewed holes, smell of urine near the nest site; large, hard, cylindrical, dark brown-to-black droppings, deposited along trails

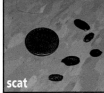
scat

Activity: nocturnal; active year-round, can be active on cloudy days

Tracks: hind paw 1½" (4 cm) long with a narrow heel and 5 toes, forepaw 1" (2.5 cm) long with 4 well-spread toes; often follows the same paths over and over, making individual tracks difficult to distinguish

Stan's Notes: A rat of cities large and small as well as rural areas, including farms. This animal has greatly benefited from its association with humans. It has adapted well to city environments, feeding on discarded food and carrion. In farm settings, it eats stored food such as grain.

Also known as Common Rat, Brown Rat, Water Rat or Sewer Rat. A good swimmer and climber. Tolerates cold temperatures well. Excavates by loosening dirt with its front feet, pushes dirt under its belly, then turns and pushes dirt out with its head and front feet. Will chew through roots when they are in the way. A true omnivore, it sometimes acts like a predator, killing chickens and other small farm animals. Able to reproduce quickly, especially when food is abundant.

Has a very small territory with a high population density. Will migrate upon occasion. Large numbers have been seen leaving an area, presumably in response to overcrowding and a dwindling food supply.

Despite its common name, the Norway Rat is thought to originate from central Asia. It was introduced to different parts of the world via trading ships in the 1600-1700s and is believed to have been brought to North America in ships that transported grain in the eighteenth century. The name "Norway" actually comes from the fact this species was scientifically described in Norway.

This is the same species as the white rats used in lab experiments. While it is not the species that carried the famed bubonic plague (Black Rat, *R. rattus*), it is still is a carrier of disease and fleas and should be exterminated whenever possible. However, it is hard to trap and exterminate since its home usually has several escape exits. Due to intense human pressure for eradication (artificial selection), it has become resistant to many types of rat poisons.

Similar species on next page
69

Despite the common name "Rat," Ord's Kangaroo Rat and Hispid Cotton Rat are not actually rats or even related to the Norway Rat. The Norway Rat is an Old World species of rat that came to North America with the early settlers. The Ord's and the Hispid are closely related to pocket mice. Both are usually found on sandy soils in grasslands and prairies. They feed mostly on seeds, but will also eat insects to supplement their diet.

The common name "Kangaroo" describes the hopping movement of an Ord's using its hind feet together (bipedal locomotion). Unlike pocket mice, which are not good jumpers, the Ord's can jump several feet when fleeing predators.

Ord's Kangaroo Rat 4-6"

Hispid Cotton Rat 6-8½"

Southern Red-backed Vole

Clethrionomys gapperi

Family: Rats and Mice (Muridae)

Size: L 3-4" (7.5-10 cm); T 1-2" (2.5-5 cm)

Weight: 1-1½ oz. (28-43 g)

Description: A rusty red back with lighter brown sides. Black belly hair with white tips, making belly appear silvery white. Rounded snout. Small round ears. Small dark eyes. Short tail.

Origin/Age: native; 1-2 years

Compare: Smaller than Meadow Vole (pg. 77), which has a more grizzled appearance and is not as red. Also smaller than Prairie Vole (pg. 77), which is gray brown with no red. Voles have shorter, rounder snouts and shorter tails than mice.

Habitat: coniferous forests, spruce bogs, swamps, wetlands, mountain regions, elevations up to 10,000' (3,050 m)

Home: nest with a hollow center, made of plant material, 3-4" (7.5-10 cm) wide, beneath a log or among tree roots

Food: insectivore, herbivore; insects, green leaves, fruit, seeds, leaf buds, bark of young trees, fungi

Sounds: inconsequential; rarely, if ever, heard

Breeding: late winter to late autumn mating; 17-19 days gestation

Young: 2-8 (average 5) offspring several times per year; born naked and toothless with eyes closed, body covered with fine hair and eyes open by about 12 days, weaned and on its own at about 3 weeks, appears gray until 1-2 months, then turns red

73

Signs: runways in grass leading beneath rocks, cut grass piled up along runways

Activity: diurnal, nocturnal; active year-round, rests and sleeps for several hours, then is active for several hours throughout the day with peaks at dawn and dusk

Tracks: hind paw ¾" (2 cm) long with 5 toes, forepaw slightly smaller with 4 toes; individual tracks are indistinguishable and create a single groove

Stan's Notes: This very common vole is a member of the Voles and Lemmings (Arvicolinae) subfamily, which is in the Rats and Mice (Muridae) family. While its common name is Southern Red-backed Vole, the species ranges from Colorado northward, across southern Canada and coastal Alaska. The Northern Red-backed Vole (not shown) looks similar and is found in northern Canada and Alaska.

The Southern Red-backed Vole is a food staple for Short-tailed Weasels (pg. 207), foxes, coyotes and many other mammals. It is also a major food item for many hawk and owl species.

A short-lived animal, with most living only 10-12 months; some, however, can survive as long as 24 months. Populations peak in autumn, with numbers dropping quickly during winter due to predation and starvation. Entire birds of prey populations may move when Southern Red-backed Vole populations drop.

Active day and night and does not hibernate. Carries on with life underneath snow (subnivean), even expanding its home range in that environment. Will follow well-maintained surface trails only occasionally, as does the Meadow Vole (pg. 77). May use tunnel systems of larger animals. Rarely enters homes or cabins. May store roots, shoots and fungi for later consumption. Underground fungi is an important and much sought food source.

Like all other vole species, the digestive tract of this species has a large pouch called a cecum, which contains microscopic bacteria (microflora). These microflora help to break down items that are hard to digest such as cellulose, which is the chief component of green plants.

Becomes sexually mature at 5-6 months. The male will stay with the family until the young are weaned.

Similar species on next page

All vole species in Colorado have stocky bodies, blunt noses and usually are dark in color. They are considered an essential component of many ecosystems in the state, with larger mammals to birds of prey relying on healthy populations of voles as a food source.

All species of voles have naked tails. Except for the Long-tailed Vole and Muskrat, they also have very short tails. Excluding the Prairie Vole and Montane Vole, they are generally found in the western half of the state in higher elevations. Mexican Voles occur only in a few locations along the southern border of Colorado.

Sagebrush Vole 3¾-4½"

Meadow Vole 4-5"

Prairie Vole 4-5"

Mexican Vole 3¾-5½"

Montane Vole 4¼-5½"

Long-tailed Vole 4¼-5½"

Not pictured: Heather Vole 4¼-5½"

Muskrat
Ondatra zibethicus

Family: Rats and Mice (Muridae)

Size: L 8-12" (20-30 cm); T 7-12" (18-30 cm)

Weight: 1-4 lb. (.5-1.8 kg)

Description: Glossy dark brown, lighter on the sides and belly. Long naked tail, covered with scales and slightly vertically flattened (taller than it is wide). Small round ears. Tiny eyes.

Origin/Age: native; 3-10 years

Compare: Much smaller with a longer, thinner tail than the American Beaver (pg. 83), which has a large flat tail. Similar habitat as the Mink (pg. 219), which has a well-furred tail and a white patch on chin.

Habitat: ponds, lakes, ditches, small rivers, elevations up to 10,000' (3,050 m)

Home: small den, called a lodge, made of cattail leaves and other soft green (herbaceous) plant material, 1-2 underwater entrances, often has 1 chamber, sometimes a burrow in a lakeshore, larger dens may have 2 chambers with separate occupants

Food: herbivore, carnivore to a much lesser extent; aquatic plants, roots, cattail and bulrush shoots, roots and rhizomes; also eats dead fish, crayfish, clams, snails and baby birds

Sounds: inconsequential; chewing sounds can be heard when feeding above water on feeding platform

Breeding: Apr-Aug mating; 25-30 days gestation

Young: 6-7 offspring 2-3 times per year; born naked with eyes closed, swims at about 2 weeks, weaned at about 3 weeks

79

swimming

lodge

Signs: well-worn trails through vegetation along a lakeshore near a muskrat lodge, feeding platform made of floating plant material, 2' square (154.8 sq. cm), usually strewn with partially eaten cattails and other plants; lodge made of mud and cut vegetation, occasionally many lodges will dot the surface of a shallow lake

Activity: nocturnal, crepuscular; active all year, doesn't hibernate

Tracks: hind paw 2½-3½" (6-9 cm) long with 5 toes and a long heel, forepaw about half the size with 5 toes spread evenly; hind paws fall near or onto fore prints (direct register) when walking, often obliterating the forepaw tracks; prints may show only 4 toes since the fifth toe is not well formed, often has a tail drag mark

Stan's Notes: This animal is native only to North America, but it has been introduced all over the world. The musky odor (most evident in the male during breeding season) emanating from two glands near the base of the rat-like tail gives it the common name. Some say the common name is a derivation of the Algonquian Indian word *musquash*, which sounds somewhat like "muskrat."

Mostly aquatic, the muskrat is highly suited to living in water. It has a waterproof coat that protects it from frigid temperatures. Partially webbed hind feet and a fringe of hair along each toe help propel the animal. The tail, which is slightly flattened vertically, also helps with forward motion and is used as a rudder. Its mouth can close behind the front teeth only, allowing the animal to cut vegetation free while it is submerged.

A good swimmer that swims backward and sideways with ease. Able to stay submerged for up to 15 minutes. Surfaces to eat. May store some roots and tubers in mud below the water to consume during winter.

When small areas of a lake open up in winter, it will often sit on the ice to feed or sun itself. Although it lives in small groups, there is no social structure and individuals act mainly on their own. Becomes sexually mature the first spring after its birth.

Lodge building seems to concentrate in the fall. Not all muskrats build a mound-type lodge. Many dig a burrow in a lakeshore. A muskrat lodge is not like a beaver lodge, which is made with woody plant material. There is only one beaver lodge per lake or stream, while there are often several muskrat lodges in a body of water. Does not defecate in the lodge, so the interior living space of the lodge is kept remarkably clean.

Overcrowding can occur in fall and winter, causing individuals to travel great distances in spring to establish new homes. Many muskrats are killed when crossing roads during this season.

American Beaver
Castor canadensis

Family: Beavers (Castoridae)

Size: L 3-4' (1-1.2 m); T 7-14" (18-36 cm)

Weight: 20-60 lb. (9-27 kg)

Description: Reddish brown fur. Body often darker than head. Large, flat, naked black tail, covered with scales. Small round ears. Large, exposed orange incisors. Tiny eyes.

Origin/Age: native; 10-15 years

Compare: Much larger than Muskrat (pg. 79), which has a long narrow tail. Look for a large flat tail to help identify the American Beaver.

Habitat: rivers, streams, ponds, lakes, ditches, elevations up to 10,000' (3,050 m) where trees and water are present

Home: den, called a lodge, hollow inside with holes on top for ventilation, 1-2 underwater entrances; beavers that live on rivers often dig burrows in riverbanks rather than constructing dens

Food: herbivore; soft bark, inner bark, aquatic plants, green leaves

Sounds: loud slap created by hitting the surface of water with the tail before diving when alarmed, chewing or gnawing sounds when feeding or felling trees

Breeding: Jan-Mar mating; 120 days gestation

Young: 1-8 kits once per year; about 1 lb. (.5 kg); born well furred with eyes open, able to swim within 1 week

tail slap

lodge

scat

Signs: dam and lodge made from large woody branches can indicate current or former activity since structures remain well after the beaver has moved on or been killed, chewed tree trunks with large amounts of wood chips at the base of trees, flattened paths through vegetation leading to and from a lake; oval pellets, 1" (2.5 cm) long, containing sawdust-like material and bark, scat seldom on land

Activity: nocturnal, crepuscular; active year-round, even under ice and when in lodge during winter

Tracks: hind paw 5" (13 cm) long with 5 toes pointing forward and a long narrow heel, forepaw 3" (7.5 cm) with 5 splayed toes; wide tail drag mark often wipes out paw prints

Stan's Notes: Largest member of the Rodent order in Colorado. Body is well suited for swimming. Valves close off the ears and nostrils when underwater, and a clear membrane covers the eyes. Can remain submerged up to 15 minutes. Webbed toes on hind feet help it swim as fast as 6 mph (10 km/h). Special lips seal the mouth yet leave the front incisors exposed, allowing it to carry branches in its mouth without water getting inside. At the lodge, it eats the soft bark of smaller branches the same way we eat corn on the cob. Doesn't eat the interior wood. Stores branches for winter use by sticking them in mud on a lake or river bottom.

Has a specialized claw on each hind foot that is split like a comb and is used for grooming. Secretes a pungent oily substance (castor) from glands near the base of its tail. Castor is used to mark territories or boundaries called castor mounds.

Monogamous and mates for life. However, will take a new mate if partner is lost. Can live up to 20 years in captivity.

Young remain with parents through their first winter. They help cut and store a winter food source and maintain the dam while parents raise another set of young. Young disperse at two years.

Builds a dam to back up a large volume of water, creating a pond. Cuts trees at night by gnawing trunks. Uses larger branches to construct the dam and lodge. Cuts smaller branches and twigs of felled trees into 6-foot (1.8 m) sections. Dam repair is triggered by the sound of moving water, not by sight. Most repair activity takes place at night.

No other mammal besides humans changes its environment as much as beavers. Beaver ponds play an important role in moose populations. Moose feed on aquatic plants, cool themselves and escape biting insects in summer in beaver ponds. Other animals, such as frogs and turtles, and many bird species including ducks, herons and egrets also benefit from the newly created habitat.

Big Brown Bat
Eptesicus fuscus

Family: Bats (Vespertilionidae)

Size: L 2-3" (5-7.5 cm); T 1½-2" (4-5 cm)

Weight: ½-⁹⁄₁₀ oz. (14-26 g)

Description: Overall brown. Dark, membranous naked wings and tail. Lighter brown belly. Dark, oval naked ears with a short round tragus. Bright black eyes. Pointed snout.

Origin/Age: native; 15-20 years

Compare: Little Brown Bat (pg. 90) is nearly identical, but smaller and winter roosts in caves. Big Brown Bat tends to winter roost in buildings such as homes.

Habitat: wide variety such as deciduous forests, suburban areas, elevations up to 10,000' (3,050 m)

Home: walls and attics of homes, churches, barns and other buildings year-round, maternity colonies also in hollow trees, will winter in mines, tunnels and caves, but little is known about these sites

Food: insectivore; small to large flying insects

Sounds: rapid series of high-pitched clicking noises, high-pitched squeaks of pups calling persistently to mother after she leaves to feed can be heard from a distance up to 30' (9.1 m) away

Breeding: Aug-Sep mating before hibernation; 60-62 days gestation; sperm stored in the reproductive tract until the spring following mating

Young: 1-2 (usually 2) pups once per year from May to July; one-third the weight of mother, born breach and naked with eyes closed, flies at 28-35 days

Signs: piles of dark brown-to-black scat under roosting sites

Activity: nocturnal; active only on warm dry nights, comes out approximately 30 minutes after sunset, feeds until full, roosts the rest of night, returns to daytime roost before sunrise

scat

Tracks: none

Stan's Notes: A common bat in Colorado, seen in many habitats from forests to cities up to 10,000 feet (3,050 m) in elevation. Found across North America from Maine to Washington and south to Florida and Central America.

Studies show that this species feeds on many crop and forest pests and insects, making it one of America's most beneficial animals and very desirable to have around. It is a fast-flying bat, reaching speeds of up to 25 mph (40 km/h), with an erratic flight pattern, evident as it swoops and dives for mosquitoes, beetles and other flying insects. Often forages over rivers and lakes, beneath streetlights or wherever large groups of flying insects congregate. Emits a high-frequency (27-48 kHz) sound (inaudible to humans) to locate prey and listens for returning echoes (echolocation). Most of these bats catch and eat one insect every three seconds, consuming $\frac{1}{10}$ ounce (3 g) per hour. During summer, when rapidly growing pups demand increasing amounts of milk, a lactating female can consume up to $\frac{7}{10}$ ounce (20 g) of insects every night, which is nearly equal to her own body weight.

Rarely winters in caves, preferring to hibernate alone or with others in small groups. Males are generally solitary during spring and summer.

Females will gather in maternity colonies of up to 75 individuals. Loyal to these maternal roosts, females return to them year after year. Approximately 80 percent of females give birth to two pups at the maternal roosts in spring and early summer.

A mother does not carry her pups during flight, but leaves them clinging to the roost until she returns. Holds pups to her chest under a wing to nurse. Recognizes young by their vocalizations.

Homeowners frequently discover these bats when remodeling or adding onto their homes during winter months. Any unwanted bat found in homes should be professionally moved or removed to avoid hurting the animal.

Similar species on next page 89

Colorado has 18 species of bats, some common, others rare. All bats in Colorado eat insects and sleep during the day. Due to the air cooling at night, most species in the state are active only during the first four hours after sunset.

The Big Brown Bat and Little Brown Bat are found in almost all habitats. Other species occur only in specific habitats. Colorado represents the northern limit of many species.

While some species migrate each fall, others remain in Colorado and hibernate. Some speculate there may be more species of bats moving in and out of the state that haven't been observed.

Little Brown Bat 1½-2"

Western Small-footed Myotis 2-2½"

Fringed Myotis 2-2¼"

Western Pipistrelle 2-2¾"

Brazilian Free-tailed Bat 2¼-2½"

Red Bat 2-3"

Silver-haired Bat 2-3"

California Myotis 2-3"

Townsend's Big-eared Bat 2½-3"

Spotted Bat 2½-3"

Yuma Myotis 2½-3"

Long-eared Myotis 2¾-3"

Allen's Big-eared Bat 2¾-3"

Hoary Bat 2-4"

Long-legged Myotis 3-3½"

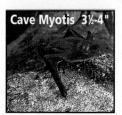
Cave Myotis 3½-4"

Big Free-tailed Bat 4¼-5½"

Least Chipmunk
Tamias minimus

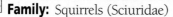

Family: Squirrels (Sciuridae)

Size: L 3-4" (7.5-10 cm); T 3-4" (7.5-10 cm)

Weight: 2-2¼ oz. (57-64 g)

Description: Overall brown fur with alternating dark and light stripes from nose to base of tail. Orange brown sides with a lighter brown rump. Chin, chest and belly are pale white to gray. Long orange brown tail, nearly the length of the body, usually with a thin dark line running the entire length.

Origin/Age: native; 2-4 years

Compare: Colorado Chipmunk (pg. 101) has lighter side (lateral) stripes. Chipmunks (pp. 97-109) look similar, so use the range maps to help identify.

Habitat: rocky outcrops, cliffs, roadsides, dry and open coniferous forests, elevations up to 10,000' (3,050 m) and higher

Home: burrow, entrance usually a small round hole with no trace of excavated dirt, sometimes at the base of a rock, occasionally nests in a tree, may have different burrows in summer and winter, winter burrow is deeper underground

Food: omnivore; seeds, fruit, nuts, insects, fungi, buds, flowers, frogs, baby birds, bird eggs, small snakes

Sounds: series of distinctive high-pitched "chip" notes that sound like a small bird, similar to most other chipmunk species

Breeding: Mar-May mating; 28-30 days gestation

Young: up to 7 offspring 1-2 times per year; born naked with eyes closed, weaned at about 60 days

Signs: piles of cracked seeds and acorns and other food on a log or large rock; oblong dark brown pellets, ⅛" (.3 cm) long, often not seen and not key in identifying this species

Activity: diurnal; does not come out on cold, rainy days

Tracks: hind paw ¾-1¼" (2-3 cm) long with 5 toes, forepaw with 4 toes is about half the size of hind paw; 1 set of 4 tracks; hind paws fall in front of fore prints; tracks rarely seen since it lives in a dry rocky habitat and usually does not come out from burrow when snow is on the ground

Stan's Notes: This is the smallest and most widespread of the 22 chipmunk species seen in North America. One of five chipmunk species in Colorado. Ranges across the western half of the state, extending north up the Rocky Mountains, across all of Canada and dropping down into some northern states such as Minnesota and Wisconsin. Home range is estimated at ¼ acre (.1 ha) with overlapping boundaries.

Like the other chipmunks, this one has fur-lined internal cheek pouches for carrying food, dirt and other items while it excavates tunnels. Often runs with its tail held vertically, like the antenna of a dune buggy. When it is on a sun-dappled forest floor or in a rocky habitat, the bold stripes provide a great camouflage.

Comfortable climbing trees to gather seeds, buds and flowers for food. Stores large amounts of seeds, nuts and dried berries in an underground cavity. Feeds on its cache when it can't get outside due to weather. Known to steal food from neighboring "chippie" caches. One study has reported that nearly 500 acorns and 1,000 cherry pits were found in a Least Chipmunk cache.

Can become tame and even very bold, seeking people for handouts in areas with increased human contact. Often lives in close association with Colorado Chipmunks with no apparent conflict.

Doesn't add a thick layer of fat in preparation for winter. Instead, it caches food and sleeps for 1-2 weeks at a time, waking to feed. Drifts into a state of deep sleep called torpor, which includes a mild metabolic rate drop, but not to the level of true hibernation.

Matures sexually at 10-12 months. Breeding season begins in late March or early April and lasts only a few weeks, depending on elevation. In high elevations, breeding season may start as late as July. Female can have up to two litters each breeding season, but this is not common.

Hopi Chipmunk
Tamias rufus

Family: Squirrels (Sciuridae)

Size: L 3¼-4" (8-10 cm); T 3-4" (7.5-10 cm)

Weight: 2-2¼ oz. (57-64 g)

Description: Pale gray to pale orange. Indistinct darker orange and white stripes on back (dorsal) from shoulders to rump. Dark orange stripe through eyes. Gray cheeks. White chin, chest, belly, nearly white feet, often a white spot behind ears. Long tail, nearly the length of body, orange to brown, black-tipped.

Origin/Age: native; 2-4 years

Compare: Colorado Chipmunk (pg. 101) has more distinct dorsal stripes. The Cliff Chipmunk (pg. 105) is overall darker and has a fluffier tail. Look for the pale gray fur and indistinct stripes on the back to help identify. Seen mainly in western Colorado, so also use range to help identify.

Habitat: canyons, rocky outcrops, cliffs, juniper and other forests, elevations up to 7,000' (2,135 m)

Home: burrow, small round entrance hole with no trace of excavated dirt, may have summer and winter burrows, winter burrow is deeper underground

Food: omnivore; seeds, fruit, nuts, insects, fungi, buds, flowers, carrion

Sounds: series of high-pitched "chips" given while flipping its tail, most chipmunk species sound similar

Breeding: Feb-Mar mating; 30-33 days gestation

Young: 2-6 offspring once per year; born naked with eyes closed, eyes open at 30 days, emerges at 40 days, weaned at 55 days, mature at 11 months

97

Signs: piles of open seeds at favorite feeding spots on prominent rocks and logs; oblong dark brown pellets, ⅛" (.3 cm) long, often not seen and not key in identifying this species

Activity: diurnal; most active in midmorning and midafternoon, seen running over and along large rocks; does not come out on cold, rainy days

Tracks: hind paw 1¼" (3 cm) long with 5 toes, forepaw with 4 toes is about half the size of hind paw; 1 set of 4 tracks; hind paws fall in front of fore prints; tracks rarely seen since it lives in a dry rocky habitat and usually does not come out from burrow when snow is on the ground

Stan's Notes: By far the most pale of the five chipmunk species in Colorado. Restricted range to the western third of the state, but the most common chipmunk in the slickrock pinyon-juniper country in western Colorado, residing at lower elevations. Seems to prefer broken rocks or rubble at the base of cliffs (talus fields) and does not range far from these areas. Active from late February through November, making it the most active chipmunk species in the state.

Was once considered the same species as Colorado Chipmunk (pg. 101), but these species apparently do not interbreed where their ranges overlap.

Highly associated with coniferous forests, especially juniper and pinyon, feeding heavily on cones and seeds. Stuffs its cheeks full and runs to a feeding spot, usually high rocks, where it can see in all directions while feeding. Collects and stores many items of food for winter consumption. Like other chipmunks, the Hopi has fur-lined internal cheek pouches for carrying food and other items, such as dirt, while it excavates tunnels.

Comfortable climbing trees or steep cliffs. Holds tail horizontally when running, which can help to identify. However, field marks, range and elevation should also be considered.

Colorado Chipmunk
Tamias quadrivittatus

Family: Squirrels (Sciuridae)

Size: L 3½-4¼" (9-10.5 cm); T 3½-4" (9-10 cm)

Weight: 2-2½ oz. (57-71 g)

Description: Overall orange to brown with alternating light and dark stripes from the nose almost to the base of tail. Orange brown sides and gray rump. Chin, chest and belly are white to gray. Long, darker brown tail, same length as the body.

Origin/Age: native; 2-4 years

Compare: Least Chipmunk (pg. 93) is more common, slightly smaller and has stripes going all the way to the base of its tail. Cliff Chipmunk (pg. 105) is slightly larger and has much less distinct stripes on its back (dorsal) and sides (laterals).

Habitat: rocky outcrops, canyons, foothills, dry and open forests, elevations up to 10,500' (3,200 m) in southern Colorado, below 7,000' (2,135 m) in northern Colorado and the Front Range

Home: burrow, small round entrance hole with no trace of excavated dirt, sometimes nests in a tree, may have different burrows in summer and winter, winter burrow is deeper underground

Food: omnivore; seeds, fruit, nuts, insects, fungi, buds, flowers, carrion

Sounds: series of distinctive high-pitched "chip" notes that sound like most other chipmunk species

Breeding: Apr-May mating; 30-33 days gestation

Young: 4-7 offspring once per year; born naked with eyes closed, weaned at about 42-49 days

Signs: piles of cracked seeds and acorns and other food on a log or large rock; oblong dark brown pellets, ⅛" (.3 cm) long, often not seen and not key in identifying this species

scat

Activity: diurnal; active in late morning and again in afternoon, does not come out on cold, rainy days or during winter

Tracks: hind paw 1¼" (3 cm) long with 5 toes, forepaw with 4 toes is about half the size of hind paw; 1 set of 4 tracks; hind paws fall in front of fore prints; tracks rarely seen since it lives in a dry rocky habitat and usually does not come out from burrow when snow is on the ground

Stan's Notes: One of the smaller chipmunks species in Colorado. Ranges from the southern half of the state, up a narrow band on the Front Range to the northern border. Home range is estimated to be 1 acre (.4 ha) with overlapping boundaries. Some studies show this species travels up to 5 acres (2 ha).

Like the other chipmunks, the Colorado Chipmunk has fur-lined internal cheek pouches for carrying food and other items, such as dirt, while it excavates tunnels. Often runs holding its tail in a horizontal position unlike the Least Chipmunk (pg. 93), which holds its tail vertically. Identifying the Colorado Chipmunk just by tail position is difficult, but noting it can be helpful.

Climbs trees more than other chipmunk species to gather seeds, buds and flowers for food. Stores small amounts of seeds, nuts and dried berries in an underground cavity. Feeds on its cache when it cannot get outside due to inclement weather.

Can become tame and even very bold, seeking people for handouts in areas with increased human contact. Often lives in close association with other chipmunks with no apparent conflict.

Does not add a thick layer of fat in preparation for winter. Caches food instead and sleeps for 1-2 weeks at a time, waking to feed. Drifts into a state of deep sleep called torpor, which includes a mild metabolic rate drop, but not to the level of true hibernation.

RARE

Cliff Chipmunk
Tamias dorsalis

Family: Squirrels (Sciuridae)

Size: L 4¼-5½" (10.5-14 cm); T 3¼-5" (8-13 cm)

Weight: 2-3 oz. (57-85 g)

Description: Overall gray to tan with faint stripes on the back (dorsal). Distinct white stripes above and below eyes. Dark eye line. Gray cheeks, sides and feet. Pale white chin, chest and belly. Long, fluffy, dark gray tail, nearly the length of the body.

Origin/Age: native; 2-4 years

Compare: The other chipmunks (pp. 93-109) have more distinct stripes on their sides and backs. Look for the gray sides and indistinct stripes to identify the Cliff Chipmunk. Occurs in a very limited range in the far northwestern corner of the state, so also use range to help identify.

Habitat: rocky outcrops, cliffs, roadsides, coniferous forests, elevations up to 9,000' (2,745 m)

Home: burrow, often under rocks or in cliff faces, small round entrance hole with no excavated dirt, winter burrow is deeper than summer burrow

Food: omnivore; seeds, fruit, nuts, insects, fungi, buds, flowers, carrion

Sounds: series of distinctive high-pitched barks (up to 100 times per minute) given while flipping its tail, most chipmunk species sound similar

Breeding: Apr-May mating; 28-30 days gestation

Young: 4-8 offspring once per year; born naked with eyes closed, emerges from burrow at 35-45 days, weaned at about 60 days

Signs: piles of cracked seeds and acorns and other food on a log or large rock; oblong dark brown pellets, ⅛" (.3 cm) long, often not seen and not key in identifying this species

Activity: diurnal; does not come out on cold, rainy days

Tracks: hind paw 1¼" (3 cm) long with 5 toes, forepaw with 4 toes is about half the size of hind paw; 1 set of 4 tracks; hind paws fall in front of fore prints; tracks rarely seen since it lives in a dry rocky habitat and usually does not come out from burrow when snow is on the ground

Stan's Notes: This chipmunk has a restricted range in the state to the far northwestern corner in Moffat County, north and west of the Yampa and Little Snake Rivers. Its home range is estimated to be ¼ acre (.1 ha) with overlapping boundaries. Cliff Chipmunks have indistinct stripes, but inhabit dry open areas where more bold striping for camouflage is not as important as it would be in other habitats. Distribution is in Nevada, south through Arizona, western New Mexico and down into Mexico.

Like the other chipmunk species, the Cliff has fur-lined internal cheek pouches for carrying food, dirt and other items while it excavates tunnels. Groups of females may gather food together, traveling short distances and returning home with cheeks stuffed with seeds, nuts or berries.

Comfortable climbing trees to gather seeds, buds and flowers for food. Stores large amounts of seeds, nuts and dried berries in an underground cavity. Feeds on its cache when it can't get outside due to weather.

Does not add a thick layer of fat in preparation for winter. Drifts into a state of deep sleep known as torpor, which includes a mild metabolic rate drop, but not to the level of true hibernation. Sleeps for 1-2 weeks at a time, waking to feed on its cache.

Matures sexually at 10-12 months. Breeding season begins in late April or May. Young emerge from burrows at 35-45 days of age.

Uinta Chipmunk
Tamias umbrinus

Family: Squirrels (Sciuridae)

Size: L 4¾-5¼" (12-13.5 cm); T 3-4½" (7.5-11 cm)

Weight: 2-3 oz. (57-85 g)

Description: Overall light brown to brown with alternating distinct dark and white stripes from shoulders to base of tail. Stripe through both eyes, not as dark as stripes on the back. Gray cheeks. White chin, chest and belly. Nearly white feet. Long brown tail, lighter on the underside and black-tipped.

Origin/Age: native; 2-4 years

Compare: Least Chipmunk (pg. 93) is more grayish, has gray undersides and runs with tail held vertically. More brown than other chipmunks. Look for the dark stripes and also use range to help identify.

Habitat: variety of habitats from pinyon-juniper forests to shrublands, river bottoms, forest edges, talus slopes, canyons, rocky outcrops, elevations from 6,500-12,000' (1,980-3,660 m)

Home: burrow, beneath rocks, logs and shrubs, several entrances, small round entrance holes, no excavated dirt, winter burrow is deeper underground

Food: omnivore; seeds, fruit, nuts, insects, fungi, buds, flowers, carrion

Sounds: series of high-pitched "chips" given while flipping its tail, most chipmunk species sound similar

Breeding: Mar-Apr mating; 30-32 days gestation

Young: 2-6 offspring once per year; born naked with eyes closed, eyes open at 30 days, emerges at 40 days, weaned at about 55 days, mature at 11 months

Signs: piles of open seeds at favorite feeding spots on prominent rocks and logs; oblong dark brown pellets, ⅛" (.3 cm) long, often not seen and not key in identifying this species

Activity: diurnal; active most of the day, does not come out on cold, rainy days or during very hot days

Tracks: hind paw 1¼" (3 cm) long with 5 toes, forepaw with 4 toes is about half the size of hind paw; 1 set of 4 tracks; hind paws fall in front of fore prints

Stan's Notes: One of the least studied of the chipmunks. Occupies the widest variety of habitats in Colorado, but has a very limited range in the state. Lives in the north central mountains and in northwestern Colorado, occupying pinyon and juniper forests and also cottonwood and willow river bottoms. In high elevations, it is found in subalpine forests. In all of these habitats, it seems to like rocky areas or talus slopes.

Found in parts of eight western states. Unlike the usually uniform and continuous population distributions of other chipmunks, the range of the Uinta is broken into pockets of isolated populations. Has a small home range of 2 acres (.8 ha).

Seems to get along with other chipmunks and is often associated with the Golden-mantled Ground Squirrel (pg. 125). Especially tame at campgrounds, where it is known to beg for food.

Climbs trees or steep cliffs easily. Carries tail horizontally when running, which can help to identify, but range, elevation and field marks should also be considered. Has fur-lined internal cheek pouches to carry food, dirt and other items while it digs tunnels.

Caches food for winter consumption and also puts on a layer of fat, which aids in hibernation. Still, it wakes periodically during winter to feed on stored food before returning to hibernation.

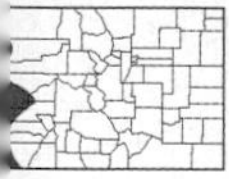

White-tailed Antelope Squirrel
Ammospermophilus leucurus

Family: Squirrels (Sciuridae)

Size: L 5½-7½" (14-19 cm); T 2-3½" (5-9 cm)

Weight: 3¾-5 oz. (106-142 g)

Description: Overall reddish brown to gray with a white side stripe from the shoulder to hip. Paler undersides. Small short ears. Small bushy tail, white below, black or dark gray on top, with a dark tip.

Origin/Age: native; 1-5 years

Compare: Golden-mantled Ground Squirrel (pg. 125) has dark side stripes and rusty red shoulders, nape and head. Wyoming Ground Squirrel (pg. 133) lacks stripes and usually is much lighter in color. Chipmunks (pp. 93-109) have striped faces.

Habitat: semideserts, shrublands, pinyon-juniper woodlands, dry rocky areas, elevations below 7,000' (2,135 m)

Home: burrow, up to 10' (3 m) long, several feet deep, no excess dirt at entrance, entrance often under shrubs or exposed, chamber lined with leaves, dried grass and bark, also uses rock crevices and abandoned animal burrows, has short escape tunnels with no chambers for emergencies only

Food: omnivore; green plants, seeds, insects, carrion, lizards, mice

Sounds: usually silent

Breeding: Feb-Apr mating; 30-35 days gestation

Young: 5-11 offspring once per year in April or May, born naked with eyes closed, independent after weaning, seen aboveground by about 5-6 weeks

113

Signs: small round entrance holes under shrubs, worn path to and from the burrow; scat is rarely seen

Activity: diurnal; most active in early morning and again in late afternoon, but can be seen during the middle of the day, usually seen running quickly back and forth to the burrow with tail held over its back, becomes much less active during long hot spells, also becomes inactive during cold, snowy parts of winter

Tracks: hind paw 1½" (4 cm) long with 5 toes, forepaw ¾" (2 cm) long with 4 toes; tracks usually seen around burrow entrance in dry sandy soils and dirt

Stan's Notes: Called White-tailed Antelope Squirrel due to the flashy white underside of its tail, similar to that of a much larger mammal, the Pronghorn Antelope (not shown). Runs very fast, like an antelope, carrying its tail over its rump. Almost always holds its tail over its back.

The most widespread of the antelope squirrels seen in many parts of southwestern states. At the northeastern edge of its range in Colorado. Seen only in far western parts of the state in elevations below 7,000 feet (2,135 m).

Home range is up to 3 acres (1.2 ha), with daily travels covering less than half that area. Seldom sits still. Instead, it races around its territory, gathering food and nesting material and returning to its burrow. Feeds on green vegetation, seeds, insects, small lizards and occasionally on smaller mammals. Digs its own burrow or takes residency in the burrow of other ground-dwelling species such as kangaroo rats or other ground squirrels.

Tolerates heat much better than cold. Spreads out on the floor of its burrow with its sparsely furred belly on the earth to cool itself. When out of the burrow, it also seeks shade during hot periods of the day.

Most active during morning and again in late afternoon. Becomes inactive in very hot or cold weather. Suns itself on rocks during winter. Retreats to its burrow in extremely cold weather, but it is thought not to hibernate.

Spotted Ground Squirrel
Xerospermophilus spilosoma

Family: Squirrels (Sciuridae)

Size: L 5-8½" (13-22 cm); T 2-3½" (5-9 cm)

Weight: 3-5 oz. (85-142 g)

Description: Overall gray to brown with many faint whitish spots, more pronounced on the hind quarter of back. White-to-tan belly. Small round ears that don't stand erect. Short thin tail, covered with hair, often with a dark tip.

Origin/Age: native; 1-4 years

Compare: Chipmunks (pp. 93-109) are smaller and have striping on their bodies and faces. White-tailed Antelope Squirrel (pg. 113) is a similar size, but lacks spots. Franklin's Ground Squirrel (pg. 129) is larger, two-toned in color and has a much larger, fluffier tail.

Habitat: dry grasslands, sandy soils, grazed fields, low elevations below 5,000' (1,525 m)

Home: burrow, up to 20' (6.1 m) long, several feet deep, no excess dirt at the entrance, burrow system has many side tunnels and chambers and several entrances, main entrance is often under shrubs, chambers are lined with leaves and dried grass

Food: omnivore; mainly green plants; also eats seeds, lizards, baby mice, insects and carrion

Sounds: usually silent, gives an alarm call

Breeding: Apr-May mating; 27-28 days gestation

Young: 5-12 offspring 1-2 times per year, born naked with eyes closed, seen aboveground by about 4-5 weeks

117

Signs: small round entrance holes under shrubs, well-worn path to and from the burrow or to a secondary burrow

Activity: diurnal; active during midday with peak activity in late morning and late afternoon, usually seen running quickly back and forth to burrow, often standing upright in fields and meadows

Tracks: hind paw 1¼" (3 cm) long with 5 toes, forepaw ½" (1 cm) long with 4 toes; tracks usually seen around burrow entrance in dry sandy soils and dirt

Stan's Notes: Fairly common ground squirrel in Colorado. Often associated with Thirteen-lined Ground Squirrels (pg. 121), which are also seen in the eastern half of the state. Not widespread, but occurs more locally where it can find suitable habitat, often where cattle are grazed.

Prefers deep sandy soils with sparse vegetation and seems to be associated with silvery wormwood, a common shrubby plant. Less omnivorous than the Thirteen-lined, but still consumes a fair amount of insects, lizards and any carrion it can find.

Males have larger home ranges than females, from ¼-1 acre (.1-.4 ha). Maintains several burrows, often having a well-worn path on the ground between the burrows and 2-3 entrance holes at the base of a shrub.

One study showed that the aboveground activities of the Spotted Ground Squirrel typically are feeding and foraging (66 percent), altered behavior such as standing and looking about (15 percent), investigating (6 percent) and sunbathing, grooming and other behaviors (8 percent). Active all year in areas of its range where winter is not severe.

Adult males in Colorado begin to hibernate in late July and early August, with females following shortly after. Juveniles stay active until September. Comes out of hibernation in Colorado in mid-April. Will remain in its burrow during the hottest part of the day in the heat of summer.

Thirteen-lined Ground Squirrel
Ictidomys tridecemlineatus

Family: Squirrels (Sciuridae)

Size: L 6-8" (15-20 cm); T 2-5" (5-13 cm)

Weight: 4-9 oz. (113-255 g)

Description: Long narrow brown body with 13 alternating tan and dark brown stripes from nape to base of tail. Small tan spots in the dark stripes. Short round ears. Large dark eyes. Short legs. Thin hairy tail, one-third the length of body.

Origin/Age: native; 1-3 years

Compare: Larger than Least Chipmunk (pg. 93), which lacks spots on its stripes and has stripes on its face. The Franklin's Ground Squirrel (pg. 129) is larger and lacks spotted stripes on its back.

Habitat: fields, lawns, pastures, meadows, prairies, along roads, cemeteries

Home: burrow, up to 20' (6.1 m) long and often only several feet deep, with a hibernation chamber beneath the frost line and no excess dirt at the entrance, many side tunnels and several entrance and exit holes; will plug entrances and exits each night with plant material

Food: omnivore; green plants, seeds, insects, bird eggs, baby mice

Sounds: trill-like whistles when threatened or alarmed

Breeding: usually April mating; 27-28 days gestation

Young: 6-12 offspring once per year in May; born naked with eyes closed, becomes independent after it is weaned, seen aboveground by about 6 weeks

121

juveniles

Signs: small round entrance holes in grass, runways 2" (5 cm) wide worn in grass (made by its low-slung body and short legs) leading to and from the holes; scat is rarely seen since the animal often defecates in its burrow or in tall grass

Activity: diurnal; most active a couple of hours after sunrise and through midday, retires to its burrow 1-2 hours before sunset, does not come out on cold, windy or rainy days, rarely comes out when snow is on the ground

Tracks: hind paw 1½" (4 cm) long with 5 toes, forepaw 1 (2.5 cm) long with 4 toes; tracks usually seen around burrow entrance

Stan's Notes: Not a gopher, but sometimes called Striped Gopher. Also called Federation Squirrel due to the pattern of stripes with spots on its body that resemble the U.S. Stars and Stripes.

When there is frequent human contact at places such as roadside rest areas and golf courses, it can be friendly and is usually tame. Semisocial, interacting with other ground squirrels during the day when feeding. Individuals have separate burrows, but live in large colonies. Colonies are not highly organized and may result from a reduction in available habitat.

A fast runner, reaching speeds up to 8 mph (13 km/h). Zigzags and turns back when pursued. Stands upright to survey its territory. Gives a trill-like whistle at the first sign of danger and runs quickly to the main burrow or one of its short, dead-end escape burrows. Often stays inside the entrance, poking its head out, repeating its alarm call.

Stores some seeds in burrow for cold or rainy days. When insects are abundant, eats more insects than plants. Adds enough body fat in summer to start hibernating in September or October. Often enters hibernation sooner than chipmunks and emerges later, making it one of the longest true hibernators in Colorado. Does not wake to feed, like chipmunks. Rolls up into a ball in the hibernation chamber. Heart rate, body temperature and respiration drop dramatically. Reduced heart rate and respiration conserve energy in winter, but still loses up to half its body weight by spring.

Male emerges from hibernation before female. Mating occurs just after female emerges, usually in April. The short breeding season may explain why the female has only one litter each year. After mating, the male does not participate in raising young.

Young often do not disperse far and dig their own burrows near their mother. This substantially increases the colony size.

Golden-mantled Ground Squirrel
Callospermophilus lateralis

Family: Squirrels (Sciuridae)

Size: L 7-9½" (18-24 cm); T 2½-4¾" (6-12 cm)

Weight: 6-14 oz. (170-397 g)

Description: Overall brown squirrel with a gray back. Reddish orange head, neck and shoulders. White and black stripes on sides. No stripes on face. Short round ears. White-to-yellow belly. Long thin tail.

Origin/Age: native; 1-4 years

Compare: Chipmunks (pp. 93-109) are smaller and have stripes on their faces. The White-tailed Antelope Squirrel (pg. 113) lacks dark stripes on its sides. Look for the reddish orange head, neck and shoulders to help identify the Golden-mantled.

Habitat: open woodlands, mountain meadows, forest edges, coniferous forests, elevations above the tree line from 5,000-12,500 feet (1,525-3,810 m)

Home: burrow, up to 25' (7.6 m) long, several feet deep, no excess dirt at the entrance, burrow system has many side tunnels and chambers and several entrances, main entrance is under logs or rocks, chambers lined with leaves, dried grass and bark

Food: omnivore; green plants, seeds, insects, carrion, small lizards, nesting birds

Sounds: variety of sharp chirps, squeals when frightened, growls when confronted

Breeding: Apr-May mating; 28-30 days gestation

Young: 2-8 offspring once per year from May to June, born naked with eyes closed, independent after weaning, aboveground by about 8-10 weeks

125

Signs: small round entrance holes under logs or rocks, worn path to and from the burrow; scat is rarely seen

Activity: diurnal; most active in early morning and again in late afternoon, but can be seen during the middle of the day, usually seen running quickly back and forth to the burrow, becomes much less active during long hot spells

Tracks: hind paw 1½" (4 cm) long with 5 toes, forepaw ¾" (2 cm) long with 4 toes; tracks usually seen around burrow entrance in dry sandy soils and dirt

Stan's Notes: The reddish orange head, neck and shoulders of the Golden-mantled give this species its common name "mantled," referring to the top part of the animal. One of the most common and widespread of ground squirrels in Colorado, seen in elevations from 5,000-12,500 feet (1,525-3,810 m). A solitary squirrel that can be rather bold. Known to beg for handouts at campgrounds and picnic areas and easily observed in many areas and habitats.

Frequently seen with other species such as chipmunks and pikas. Often mistaken for a chipmunk due to its dark and light stripes, but lacks any striping on its face or head. Takes dust baths to help maintain its thick fur, rolling in fine grain or dry dirt.

Feeds on a variety of foods and uses its large cheek pouches to carry food back to its burrow for storage and consumption later. Each fall it puts on an extra layer of fat in preparation for winter hibernation. Males, which are slightly larger than females, add more fat at this time. During hibernation it will occasionally wake to feed on its stored food cache. Arouses every 5-7 days during hibernation, but may stay inactive for up to 14 days during the coldest, darkest part of winter. Hibernates from October to April in many parts of the region.

Franklin's Ground Squirrel
Poliocitellus franklinii

RARE

Family: Squirrels (Sciuridae)

Size: L 8-10" (20-25 cm); T 5-6" (13-15 cm)

Weight: ¾-1½ lb. (.3-.7 kg)

Description: Long, narrow brown body with gray head, neck, chest and belly. Black-tipped hair, producing a peppered appearance. Small round ears and dark eyes. Prominent white ring around each eye. Long light gray tail, moderately furred.

Origin/Age: native; 1-4 years

Compare: The Thirteen-lined Ground Squirrel (pg. 121) is shorter and has 13 alternating tan and dark stripes. Look for the bold white ring around each eye and unique gray and brown coloration to help identify the Franklin's Ground Squirrel.

Habitat: brushy fields, scrubby meadows, prairies, lawns, roadside rest areas, cemeteries, campgrounds, picnic areas, elevations below 5,000' (1,525 m)

Home: burrow, up to 20' (6 m) long and several feet deep, there is often no excavated dirt at concealed entrance holes, hibernation chamber frequently below the frost line and filled with dried grasses

Food: omnivore; green plants, seeds, berries, insects, baby mice and other small mammals, small birds, bird eggs, toads, frogs

Sounds: whistle-like trills when frightened

Breeding: Apr-May mating; 26-28 days gestation

Young: 2-12 offspring once per year; emerges from the burrow at 30-35 days and will begin to follow the mother several days later

Signs: well-worn runways through tall grass, often hard to see; small, round brown pellets, ¼-½" (.6-1 cm) wide, not often seen

Activity: diurnal; spends most of its life underground, most active aboveground on warm sunny days

Tracks: hind paw 1½-1¾" (4-4.5 cm) long with 5 toes, forepaw with 4 toes is about half the size of hind paw; 1 set of 4 tracks; tracks are not very common since the animal does not come out when snow is on the ground, in wet weather or when conditions are muddy

Stan's Notes: The distribution of this squirrel in Colorado is not known. No sizable population has been discovered, but specimens have been taken from just outside the state in Nebraska, Kansas and Wyoming. Many people suggest that this species is expanding its range and will populate Colorado in the very near future.

Named for Arctic explorer Sir John Franklin. The most social of ground squirrels, usually in small colonies. (Most, however, live alone in their burrows.) Populations in colonies can fluctuate from overabundant in some years to seemingly nonexistent in others.

A friendly squirrel, very accustomed to people. Usually seen at roadside rest areas and picnic grounds. Prefers brushy or open wooded areas. Stands on its hind legs to survey the surroundings. Gives a whistle-like trill when alarmed and runs to its burrow.

A true omnivore and the most carnivorous of ground squirrels, eating a wide range of small mammals. Breaks open eggs, usually those of ground-dwelling birds, curling its body around the egg, bracing it with its hind feet and biting through the shell. Will also eat just about anything fed to it by people.

Will nearly double its springtime body weight in preparation for hibernation, losing the weight during the winter months. A true hibernator, entering hibernation in September or October and emerging in April or May. Male comes out of hibernation about a week before the female and mates days after the female emerges.

Wyoming Ground Squirrel

Urocitellus elegans

Family: Squirrels (Sciuridae)

Size: L 8-11" (20-28 cm); T 3-4" (7.5-10 cm)

Weight: 10-15 oz. (284-425 g)

Description: An overall tan squirrel with scattered gray flecks, lighter below, and a gray face. Small round ears that don't stand erect. Long thin tail with a light brown underside and dark (sometimes light) tip.

Origin/Age: native; 1-4 years

Compare: Larger than all chipmunks (pp. 93-109), which have stripes on their bodies and faces. White-tailed Antelope Squirrel (pg. 113) is smaller and has a white underside of tail. Franklin's Ground Squirrel (pg. 129) has a similar size, but is two-toned in color and has a much larger, fluffier tail.

Habitat: grasslands, sagebrush, meadows, elevations from 6,000-12,000' (1,830-3,660 m)

Home: burrow, up to 25' (7.6 m) long, several feet deep, no excess dirt at the entrance, burrow system has many side tunnels and chambers and several entrances, main entrance is under logs or rocks, chambers lined with leaves, dried grass and bark

Food: herbivore; green plants, flowers, seeds, fruit

Sounds: very weak, high-pitched alarm call, twitters and trills when retreating to burrow

Breeding: Mar-Apr mating; 22-24 days gestation

Young: 3-11 offspring once per year in May or June, born naked with eyes closed, independent after weaning, seen aboveground by about 4-5 weeks

Signs: small round entrance holes near tufts of grass, worn path to and from the burrow

Activity: diurnal; active all day with peak activity in midmorning and late afternoon, usually seen running quickly back and forth to the burrow, often standing upright in fields and meadows, flicking its tail, gathering food, chasing or fighting

Tracks: hind paw 1½" (4 cm) long with 5 toes, forepaw ¾" (2 cm) long with 4 toes; tracks usually seen around burrow entrance in dry sandy soils and dirt

Stan's Notes: An active ground squirrel that is often seen in fairly large colonies in open or grassy mountain meadows. Individuals live alone in their own burrow system. Males may defend a small territory during breeding season, which is early spring. Females maintain territories directly around the burrow entrance.

Spends more time aboveground than most of the other ground squirrels. One study showed that 40 percent of its aboveground activity is spent feeding, 36 percent is spent in an alert, upright posture and less than 5 percent includes all other activities. Often stands upright, which led to another common name, Picket Pins, describing its resemblance to a stake in the ground that tethers an animal.

The alarm call of this species is so weak in volume, it is hard to determine the point of origin. Calls are frequently made from the hidden entrance of its burrow, making it difficult to spot.

An early hibernator, with some individuals hibernating as early as July and August in high elevations. Most hibernation, however, starts in September in Colorado. Males emerge from hibernation 1-2 weeks before the females. Mating occurs in March or April, within a week of emerging from hibernation.

Young are seen aboveground in just 4-5 weeks. At the end of the first summer, they are dispersed away from their parents to their own burrows, where they spend the winter hibernating on their own. Becomes sexually mature after the first winter.

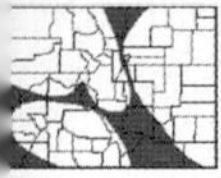

Rock Squirrel

Otospermophilus variegatus

Family: Squirrels (Sciuridae)

Size: L 11-13" (28-33 cm); T 6-8" (15-20 cm)

Weight: 1-2 lb. (.5-.9 kg)

Description: Long, narrow brown (sometimes brown-to-rust) body mottled with gray to tan. White ring around the eyes. Short round ears. Short legs. Long, thick bushy tail.

Origin/Age: native; 1-5 years

Compare: Larger, thicker and has a much larger, bushier tail than Wyoming Ground Squirrel (pg. 133). The Franklin's Ground Squirrel (pg. 129) lacks mottling and has a smaller tail. The Fox Squirrel (pg. 153) looks similar, but is a tree dweller.

Habitat: rocky fields and hillsides, canyons, talus fields, shrublands, elevations below 8,300' (2,530 m)

Home: burrow, up to 20' (6.1 m) long and often only several feet deep, no excess dirt at the entrance, many side tunnels and several entrance and exit holes, chamber lined with leaves, dried grass and especially tree bark stripped from the tree line

Food: omnivore; green plants, seeds, insects, fruit, nuts, bird eggs, baby mice, baby rabbits, carrion

Sounds: usually silent, females give a sharp clear whistle followed by a low-pitched trill when threatened or alarmed

Breeding: usually April mating; 27-28 days gestation

Young: 3-9 offspring once per year in April, born naked with eyes closed, becomes independent after it is weaned, seen aboveground by about 8-10 weeks

137

Signs: small round entrance holes under large rocks, worn path to and from the burrow; scat is rarely seen since the animal often defecates in its burrow or in dense vegetation

Activity: diurnal; most active in early morning and again in late afternoon, can be seen during the middle of the day, sometimes seen sunning itself on large rocks, will become much less active during long hot spells, also becomes inactive during the cold, snowy parts of winter

Tracks: hind paw 2¼" (5.5 cm) long with 5 toes, forepaw 1½" (4 cm) long with 4 toes; tracks often seen near burrow entrance

Stan's Notes: A squirrel of rocky hillsides, canyons, talus fields and dense vegetation below 8,300 feet (2,530 m). Can also be found in shrublands and juniper woodlands in higher elevations. Increasingly found in urban and suburban areas that have large rocks or retaining walls. Expanding its range in Colorado eastward along river corridors. Populations now extend into Fort Collins.

An expert climber, often climbing trees and bushes to find nuts and fruit. Often confused with the Fox Squirrel (pg. 153) when it is in trees. An opportunistic feeder, foraging on whatever is ripe or available at the time. Fills its large internal cheek pouches to help transport excess food back to the burrow for consumption. During the growing season, it prefers green plants and flowers. Also eats carrion, insects and other protein when available. Has been known to catch, kill and eat baby rabbits, nesting birds or bird eggs.

Apparently does not store food in its burrow like other ground squirrels. Instead, it relies on accumulated fat for survival during bad weather. In colder parts of its range, it hibernates for short durations. Remains active all year in warmer parts of its range.

Usually colonial, with dominant males defending larger areas of territory during breeding season. Dominant females push out less dominant females and also subordinate males so they can be closer to dominant males during breeding season. Rock Squirrel densities are low, with only 5-6 individuals per acre. During the non-breeding season, adults occupy individual home ranges.

Only moderately social; adults don't interact with others outside of breeding season. Individuals familiar with each other approach one another head on and touch noses. Unfamiliar squirrels will approach each other at right angles with many threat displays.

Northern Flying Squirrel
Glaucomys sabrinus

Family: Squirrels (Sciuridae)

Size: L 7-9" (18-22.5 cm); T 4-7" (10-18 cm)

Weight: 1½-3½ oz. (43-99 g)

Description: Light brown-to-gray fur above. White underside. Wide flat tail, gray above and white below. Large, bulging dark eyes. Loose fold of skin between front and hind legs.

Origin/Age: native; 2-5 years

Compare: No other flying squirrel species occurs in or near Colorado. Look for a small squirrel with large dark eyes to help identify.

Habitat: coniferous and deciduous forests

Home: nest lined with soft plant material, usually in an old woodpecker hole, sometimes in a nest box or an attic in homes and outbuildings, may build a small round nest of leaves on a tree branch

Food: omnivore; seeds, nuts, carrion, baby mice, baby birds, bird eggs, lichens, mushrooms, fungi

Sounds: faint, bird-like calls during the night, young give high-pitched squeaks

Breeding: spring mating; 40 days gestation

Young: 2-6 (average 3) offspring, usually once per year

Signs: food has mysteriously disappeared from bird feeders overnight

Activity: nocturnal; active year-round

Tracks: hind paw 1½" (4 cm) long with 5 toes, forepaw ¾" (2 cm) long with 4 toes; 1 set of 4 tracks; large landing mark (sitzmark) followed by bounding tracks, with hind paws falling in front of front prints; tracks lead to the base of a tree or suddenly appear in snow

Stan's Notes: There is no known population of flying squirrel in Colorado. However, records show small populations just north of the border at the extreme northwestern corner of the state, making it likely that this species may be found in Colorado sometime in the future.

The flying squirrel is a nocturnal animal that has large bulging eyes, enabling it to see well at night. The common name "Flying Squirrel" is a misnomer because this mammal does not have the capability to fly, only the ability to glide. In part, this is due to a large flap of skin (patagium) attached to its front and hind legs and sides of its body.

To glide, a flying squirrel will climb to the top of a tree and launch itself, extending its four legs outward and stretching the patagium to make a flat, wing-like airfoil. Its flat tail adds some additional lift and acts like a rudder to help maneuver objects while gliding. Most glides are as long as 20-50 feet (6.1-15.2 m) and terminate at the trunk of another tree. To create an air brake for a soft landing, the squirrel will quickly lift its head and tuck its tail between its hind legs. After landing, it will scamper to the opposite side of the tree trunk, presumably to avoid any flying predators that may be following.

The flying squirrel is the most carnivorous of the tree squirrels, finding, killing and eating small mice, dead flesh (carrion) and even baby birds and bird eggs. It is a gregarious animal, with many individuals living together in a nest.

Young are born helpless with eyes closed. Weaned at 5-7 weeks, they may stay with their mother through their first winter.

Most flying squirrels live only 2-5 years, but some have lived as long as 10 years in captivity. However, please don't capture these animals. Report any sighting of a flying squirrel to the Colorado Division of Wildlife.

Pine Squirrel
Tamiasciurus hudsonicus

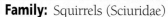

Family: Squirrels (Sciuridae)

Size: L 7-9" (18-22.5 cm); T 4-7" (10-18 cm)

Weight: 5-9 oz. (142-255 g)

Description: Overall rusty red, with brighter red fur on sides. Bright white belly. Distinctive white ring around eyes. Large, fluffy red tail with a black tip. Black line separating the red back from the white belly in summer. Tufted ears in winter.

Origin/Age: native; 2-5 years

Compare: Abert's Squirrel (pg. 149) occurs in different color morphs, but not red. Fox Squirrel (pg. 153) is dull orange to gray and has a much larger tail.

Habitat: forests, suburban and urban yards, parks, elevations from 6,000-12,000' (1,830-3,660 m)

Home: nest (drey) made mainly with grapevine bark and dried leaves, in a tree cavity (sometimes a burrow), may build a small ball-shaped nest from lichen and grass, may take a Fox Squirrel nest

Food: omnivore; pine cone seeds and other seeds, nuts, fruit, acorns, corn, mushrooms; also eats baby birds, bird eggs and carrion

Sounds: loud raspy chatters or wheezy barks when upset or threatened, may bark nonstop for up to an hour, distinctive buzz-like calls given by the male when chasing a female to mate

Breeding: Mar-Apr mating; 33-35 days gestation

Young: 2-5 offspring once per year from April to May; born naked with eyes closed, weaned and on its own after 7-8 weeks

drying
mushrooms

scat

Signs: discarded pine cone parts (midden) in a pile on the ground under a tree branch, acorns and other large nuts with a single ragged hole at one end and nutmeat missing

Activity: diurnal; active year-round, but may hole up for a couple days in the nest during very cold, hot or rainy weather

Tracks: hind paw 1½" (4 cm) long with 5 toes, forepaw ¾" (2 cm) long with 4 toes; 1 set of 4 tracks; forepaws fall side by side and behind hind prints

Stan's Notes: Known locally as Chickaree. Also known as Red Squirrel because of its reddish fur. Although small in size, the Pine Squirrel has a big attitude and is well known for chasing away larger Fox Squirrels and other small mammals. However, the success of the Pine Squirrel is a function of food resources, not feistiness.

Very common in non-coniferous habitats, but usually associated with pine trees. Feeds heavily on pine cone seeds. Cuts the cones from trees and carries them to a specific spot to eat. A large pile of discarded cone parts, known as a midden, accumulates under the perch. Caches up to a bushel of fresh cones in the midden to eat later. Large middens are usually the result of several squirrels using the same favorite perch over time, with one taking over the spot when another dies. Consumes Amanita mushrooms, which are poisonous to humans, without ill effects. Hangs mushrooms to dry on tree branches for future consumption.

Like the Fox Squirrel, it constructs leaf nests (dreys), but does not build as many. Dreys are built closer to the main trunk with more sticks and less leaves and are half the size of Fox Squirrel nests.

Several males will chase a female on tree branches prior to mating. A male may mate with more than one female, but the female is receptive to mating only once on one day in late winter or spring.

The most seasonally dimorphic of squirrels, molting in late spring and again in early autumn. Black morph and white albinos occur but are quite uncommon, unlike other squirrel species.

The genus *Tamiasciurus* is only in North America and includes one other species, Douglas Squirrel (not shown), which occurs in the Pacific Northwest. The species name *hudsonicus* was given because the Pine Squirrel ranges as far north in Canada to Hudson Bay and west across Canada and most of Alaska. In fact, it has one of the widest distributions of any squirrel in North America.

gray morph

Abert's Squirrel
Sciurus aberti

Family: Squirrels (Sciuridae)

Size: L 9-11" (22.5-28 cm); T 8-10" (20-25 cm)

Weight: 1¼-1¾ lb. (.6-1.7 kg)

Description: A wide variety of colors from gray to reddish to brown and black. Gray morph has a white chest and belly, occasionally with a white tail. Brown morph is all brown. Black morph is all black. Long "tasseled" ear tufts. Large, very fluffy tail.

Origin/Age: native; 2-5 years

Compare: Fox Squirrel (pg. 153) is larger and lacks the long ear tufts. Pine Squirrel (pg. 145) is smaller, has a smaller tail and lacks the ear tufts.

Habitat: Ponderosa Pine forests, open coniferous mountain forests, elevations above 6,000' (1,830 m)

Home: nest (drey) constructed with small sticks up to 2' (61 cm) wide, occasionally built in the midst of mistletoe infestation, chamber lined with grasses and other soft plant material, most are at least 20' (6.1 m) from the ground on the south side of a Ponderosa Pine tree, near the trunk

Food: omnivore; Ponderosa Pine tree seeds, inner bark, buds and flowers, fungi, berries, carrion

Sounds: aggressive threat calls, alarm barks, teeth chattering, screams

Breeding: Mar-Apr mating; 44-46 days gestation

Young: 2-4 offspring once per year; born with eyes closed, eyes open at about 30 days, well developed at 6 weeks, may leave mother at 9-10 weeks, remains with family several more weeks

149

black morph

brown morph

Signs: small debris pile of pine cone parts, small twigs without needles or outer bark laying about on the ground

Activity: diurnal; active all day year-round, usually begins feeding late in the morning, several hours after sunrise

Tracks: hind paw 2¾-3" (7-7.5 cm) long with 5 toes, forepaw 1½" (4 cm) long with 4 toes; 1 set of 4 tracks; forepaws fall side by side and behind hind prints

Stan's Notes: Abert's Squirrel occurs in isolated mountainous pockets in Colorado, Utah, Arizona and New Mexico. Almost always associated with Ponderosa Pine forests, being dependent on several parts of the tree for food.

A well-studied species in Colorado, known to feed in winter on the inner bark (phloem) of particular trees such as the Ponderosa Pine. Trees that are edible in winter are chemically and physiologically different from other trees in the forest, having less toxic chemicals such as monoterpenes. These trees represent less than 10 percent of all trees in a given area.

Feeds mainly on seeds during the rest of the year. It is estimated that while the Abert's eats up to 75 percent of all Ponderosa Pine seeds in a forest, there are still enough seeds left to reproduce more trees.

Uses its nest year-round, retreating there every night. Spends up to several successive days in the nest during harsh winter weather. Will store seeds on the ground, but not in the nest.

Flicks its large tail to communicate with the other squirrels, along with foot stomping. During courtship, males follow females up and down trees. These chases can go on for hours and result in copulation several times a day.

Not common in Colorado in the early 1900s, but has increased after restrictions were placed on hunting. Not very territorial and mostly solitary except during breeding season. Males have larger home ranges than females. Population trends to more males than females.

Fox Squirrel
Sciurus niger

Family: Squirrels (Sciuridae)

Size: L 10-15" (25-38 cm); T 8-13" (20-33 cm)

Weight: 1-2¼ lb. (.5-1 kg)

Description: Dark gray fur with yellow and orange highlights. Bright rusty orange chin, chest and belly. Large, fluffy, rusty orange tail. Very rare black morph has a white nose and belly and white-tipped ears.

Origin/Age: native; 2-5 years

Compare: The Pine Squirrel (pg. 145) is about half the size and lacks a large orange tail. The Abert's Squirrel (pg. 149) is smaller and has large ear tufts.

Habitat: woodlands, suburban and urban yards, parks, elevations up to 7,500' (2,285 m)

Home: leaf nest (drey) during summer, up to 2' (61 cm) wide, lined with soft plant material, usually with a side entrance, in a major fork near the main trunk of a tree, nest is in a tree cavity in winter and occupied by several individuals if enough food is available, also used for birthing; may build and use up to 6 nests

Food: omnivore; nuts, corn, pine cone seeds and other seeds, fruit, mushrooms, bird eggs, baby birds, mice, insects, carrion

Sounds: hoarse scolding call

Breeding: Jan-Feb and Jun-Jul mating; 40-45 days gestation

Young: 2-4 offspring 1-2 times per year; born with eyes closed, eyes open at about 30 days, leaves mother and on own at about 3 months

153

black morph

Signs: large debris pile of split nutshells, whole corncobs and husks strewn about underneath the feeding perch

Activity: diurnal; active year-round, usually begins feeding late in the morning, several hours after sunrise, often active during the middle of the day

Tracks: hind paw 2¾-3" (7-7.5 cm) long with 5 toes, forepaw 1½" (4 cm) long with 4 toes; 1 set of 4 tracks; forepaws fall side by side and behind hind prints

Stan's Notes: The largest of tree squirrels, with its bright rusty orange color making it easy to spot in the forest. Common name "Fox" was given for its oversized rusty orange tail, which is like that of the Red Fox. Some individuals are black with a white nose and belly and white-tipped ears, hence the species name *niger*.

Fox Squirrels spend more time farther away from trees than Pine Squirrels, searching for food on the ground and traveling, but both species collect, bury and retrieve nuts in the same way, using their sense of smell to find buried nuts. Fox Squirrels carry food back to a "regular" spot to eat. Unlike Pine Squirrels, which use nearly all available tree cavities for their nests, Fox Squirrels build large leaf nests in tree crotches.

Fox Squirrels have a large home range that is ten times larger than that of Pine Squirrels, up to 50 acres (20 ha)—so only a few Fox Squirrels are seen in any given area. They have been expanding their range in Colorado for many years and are now seen in most cities along the front range. With additional expansion up into river valleys and other tributaries penetrating the foothills, Fox Squirrels are now also found in elevations as high as 7,500 feet (2,285 m). Many current populations were the direct result of introductions made in the early 1900s, but now there is an invasion occurring from the plains to the east. While the species is much more tolerant of humans than Abert's Squirrels, it is now pushing the Abert's out of some areas.

leaf nest

On examination of its stomach contents, it rarely has tapeworms or roundworms. One explanation is that the acorns it eats have large amounts of tannin, which is highly toxic to these parasites.

Several males "chase" one female prior to mating, following her throughout the day. Female will mate with more than one male.

155

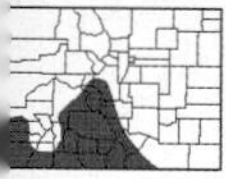

Gunnison's Prairie Dog

Cynomys gunnisoni

Family: Squirrels (Sciuridae)

Size: L 10-12½" (25-32 cm); T 2-2½" (5-6 cm)

Weight: 1-2½ lb. (.5-1.1 kg)

Description: Overall yellowish tan to cinnamon with tiny black flecks. Lighter undersides. Top of head and area just above eyes are darker than the rest of body. Small round ears that do not stand upright. Short thin tail, one-third of it white from the tip.

Origin/Age: native; 1-5 years

Compare: Overall darker than the White-tailed Prairie Dog (pg. 161), which is similar, but occurs in northwestern Colorado. The Black-tailed Prairie Dog (pg. 165) has a black-tipped tail and is more common. Wyoming Ground Squirrel (pg. 133) has a shorter tail and distinctive alarm call.

Habitat: short grass prairies, mountain valleys, elevations from 6,000-12,000' (1,830-3,660 m)

Home: extensive burrow system, up to 30' (9.1 m) long and up to 5' (1.5 m) deep, small mounds or no dirt at entrance, many side tunnels and chambers and several entrances, intertwines with neighbor burrows, dried grass lines nest chamber

Food: herbivore; grasses, sedges, roots

Sounds: variety of calls, high-pitched bark or alarm call, very similar to the White-tailed Prairie Dog

Breeding: Mar-Apr mating; 30-33 days gestation

Young: 3-8 offspring once per year, born naked with eyes closed, seen aboveground by about 4-7 weeks in June and July

Signs: several mounds of dome-shaped dirt with a single entrance hole, many burrows do not have dirt mounds

Activity: diurnal; active all day, remains underground on cold and rainy days, becomes inactive during the middle of the day in hot weather, can be seen during winter in lower elevations when weather permits

Tracks: hind paw 2-2½" (5-6 cm) long with 5 toes, forepaw 1" (2.5 cm) long with 4 toes; tracks usually seen around burrow entrance in dry sandy soils and dirt

Stan's Notes: The Gunnison's Prairie Dog is very similar to the other two prairie dog species in Colorado, but is not as common, restricted to southwestern and south central parts of the state. Like the White-tailed Prairie Dog (pg. 161), it is found in higher elevations than Black-tailed Prairie Dogs (pg. 165), with a looser aggregation of clans or families.

Like other prairie dogs, the Gunnison's does not require any free-standing water. Instead, all of its water needs are met through the green plants and roots it eats. About 60 percent of its time above-ground is spent gathering food and feeding. It gathers grasses in large amounts, storing the material in underground chambers for consumption later or for lining a nesting chamber.

Adults start to hibernate later in the year than White-tailed Prairie Dogs, entering hibernation by October. Emerges by mid-April. Hibernation may last for 4-6 months, with shorter hibernation times occurring at lower elevations.

According to results of a study, the call of the Gunnison's appears to convey specific information about the number and type of predators approaching.

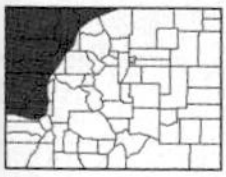

White-tailed Prairie Dog
Cynomys leucurus

Family: Squirrels (Sciuridae)

Size: L 11-13" (28-33 cm); T 2-2½" (5-6 cm)

Weight: 1½-2½ lb. (.7-1.1 kg)

Description: Uniform tan to light brown (sometimes pinkish) with cream-to-white undersides. Distinctive dark facial markings, usually above eyes, extending to cheeks. Short round ears that don't stand upright. Short thin tail with short hairs and a white tip.

Origin/Age: native; 1-5 years

Compare: Franklin's Ground Squirrel (pg. 129) has a two-toned body and a larger, furrier tail. Black-tailed Prairie Dog (pg. 165) has a black-tipped tail and is much more common. The Gunnison's Prairie Dog (pg. 157) has a gray-tipped tail, with gray extending down the sides of tail.

Habitat: semideserts, shrublands, pastures, elevations up to 10,000' (3,050 m), often 8,500' (2,590 m)

Home: extensive burrow system, up to 30' (9.1 m) long and up to 5' (1.5 m) deep, large mounds of dirt at entrance, many side tunnels and chambers, several entrances, does not intertwine with neighbor burrows, dried grass lines nest chamber

Food: herbivore; grasses, sedges, roots

Sounds: variety of calls, high-pitched bark or alarm call, very similar to the Black-tailed Prairie Dog

Breeding: Mar-Apr mating; 30-33 days gestation

Young: 4-8 offspring once per year, born naked with eyes closed, seen aboveground by about 4-7 weeks in May and June

Signs: many large volcano-shaped domes with a single entrance hole, no cut grass around the entrance

Activity: diurnal; active all day, remains underground on cold and rainy days, becomes inactive during the middle of the day in hot weather, can be seen during winter in lower elevations when weather permits

Tracks: hind paw 2-2½" (5-6 cm) long with 5 toes, forepaw 1" (2.5 cm) long with 4 toes; tracks usually seen around burrow entrance in dry sandy soils and dirt

Stan's Notes: The White-tailed Prairie Dog appears very similar to the Black-tailed Prairie Dog (pg. 165), but the White-tailed range is restricted to northwestern parts of Colorado in higher elevations than the Black-tailed occupies, up to 10,000 feet (3,050 m).

Adult White-tails do not interact with one another as much as adult Black-tails. White-tailed colonies are not as large as those of Black-tails, and their burrow systems are less extensive. Still, one White-tailed burrow was found to contain turning bays, sleeping quarters, hibernacula (places to hibernate) and a maternity area.

Unlike Black-tails, which are active all year, White-tails hibernate during winter, starting in August. By the end of summer, they will have accumulated more body fat in preparation for hibernation, which may last for perhaps 4-6 months. Regardless, White-tails also store dried grasses and other foods underground to eat if they awaken during winter.

Breeds slightly later than Black-tails, but aside from this, all other aspects of reproduction are very similar. Eats grasses during the warmer season and feeds on plant roots in inclement weather.

Black-tailed Prairie Dog
Cynomys ludovicianus

Family: Squirrels (Sciuridae)

Size: L 12-14" (30-36 cm); T 3-4½" (7.5-11 cm)

Weight: 1½-3 lb. (.7-1.4 kg)

Description: Uniform tan to light brown (sometimes cinnamon) with cream-to-white undersides. Short round ears that do not stand upright. Short, thin black-tipped tail, covered with short hairs.

Origin/Age: native; 1-4 years

Compare: Franklin's Ground Squirrel (pg. 129) has a two-toned body and a larger, furrier tail. White-tailed Prairie Dog (pg. 161) is slightly smaller and has a white-tipped tail. The Gunnison's Prairie Dog (pg. 157) is smaller, with a shorter gray-tipped tail and gray extending down the sides of tail.

Habitat: short grass prairies, fields, pastures, elevations below 6,000' (1,830 m)

Home: extensive burrow systems, up to 30' (9.1 m) long and up to 7' (2.1 m) deep, large mounds of excess dirt at entrance, many side tunnels and chambers, several entrances, some burrows are intertwined with neighbor burrows, dried grass lines the nest chamber

Food: herbivore; grasses, sedges, roots

Sounds: variety of calls, high-pitched bark or alarm call given by several individuals, one after another

Breeding: Feb-Mar mating; 30-35 days gestation

Young: 4-8 offspring once per year, born naked with eyes closed, seen aboveground by about 4-7 weeks in May and June

den entrance

barking

Signs: many large volcano-shaped domes with a single entrance hole, cut grass around the vicinity of the entrance

Activity: diurnal; active all day year-round, remains underground on extremely cold or rainy days, becomes inactive during the middle of the day in hot weather, becomes less active in winter

Tracks: hind paw 2-2½" (5-6 cm) long with 5 toes, forepaw 1" (2.5 cm) long with 4 toes; tracks usually seen around burrow entrance in dry sandy soils and dirt

Stan's Notes: Commonly seen in open fields and prairies. Makes its home in prairie dog towns, which can be large and expansive, with hundreds of mounded entrance holes dotting the landscape.

Active during the day, spending most of its time aboveground, feeding on green plants. Does not hibernate, but will stay underground for several days during inclement weather.

A prairie dog has cones in its eyes, but no rods. As a result, it does not see very well in dim light or while underground.

Reproduces only once each year, with just 30 percent of young females reproducing in their first year. Young are born naked and eyes stay closed for 5 weeks. They are fully furred by 3 weeks and fully grown by autumn. Seen aboveground in late May and June.

At first, the young don't wander far from their burrow. Gradually, as they grow, they start to explore farther away in fields. Activities include playing, chasing, play fighting, wrestling and running up to parents. Adults rarely exhibit these behaviors.

Adults mutually groom one another or touch noses, sniffing each other. An individual will stand erect at the entrance to its burrow and give a loud sharp bark at any sign of danger, throwing its head back while standing on hind legs. The bark is usually followed by other colony members echoing the call.

Despite many years of persecution, prairie dogs have managed to make a comeback and are now abundant. With the successful reintroduction of the Black-footed Ferret (pg. 223), which has a main diet of prairie dogs, prairie dog populations may once again be brought back into balance.

Yellow-bellied Marmot
Marmota flaviventris

Family: Squirrels (Sciuridae)

Size: L 15-21" (38-53 cm); T 5-8½" (13-22 cm)

Weight: 5-12 lb. (2.3-5.4 kg)

Description: Highly variable in color, from yellowish brown to shades of rust to black. Grizzled appearance with a thick body, short legs, short bushy tail and short round ears that do not stand upright. White around the muzzle and white marks on sides of neck below ears. Often has a whitish band across the nose. Male usually slightly larger than female.

Origin/Age: native; 2-7 years

Compare: Smaller than American Badger (pg. 227), which has a white stripe down the center of its head and a gray body. American Beaver (pg. 83) is larger, has a large flat tail and lives mainly in water.

Habitat: rock areas, talus slopes, cliffs, valleys, elevations from 7,000-11,000' (2,135-3,355 m)

Home: short burrow system, up to 15' (4.5 m) long and up to 5' (1.5 m) deep, entrance underneath large rocks, up to 9" (22.5 cm) wide, fan of dirt may extend out from under rocks, several side tunnels and chambers and several entrances

Food: herbivore; grasses, sedges, roots, flowers, seeds

Sounds: various calls, often gives chirp and whistle alarm calls at the entrance of burrow before retreating

Breeding: Mar-Apr mating; 30-33 days gestation

Young: 3-8 offspring once per year, born naked with eyes closed, seen aboveground by about 4-7 weeks in late June or July

Signs: fans of dirt extending out from a single entrance hole under large rocks or at a building foundation, most burrows are on slopes with a southwestern or northeastern orientation

Activity: diurnal; peak activities are in early morning and late in the afternoon, remains underground on cold and rainy days, becomes inactive during the middle of the day in hot weather

Tracks: hind paw 3-3½" (7.5-9 cm) long with 5 toes, forepaw 1¾" (4.5 cm) long with 4 toes; tracks usually not seen because of the rocky habitat

Stan's Notes: The marmot is actually a type of ground squirrel. Estimated to spend up to 80 percent of its life underground, with about three-quarters of that in hibernation. Occupies alpine tundra, where rocks are plentiful. Also known as Mountain Marmot or Rockchuck. Similar to the Woodchuck (not shown), a separate species found in the eastern half of the United States.

Often seen sitting on the edge of a large rock, sunning itself, overlooking the terrain. Sometimes beats down a well-worn path to and from its favorite feeding grounds. A strict herbivore with a preference for dandelions and other flowers. Will eat toxic plants, but apparently avoids the parts of plants where the most toxic chemicals are concentrated.

Gives a loud whistle when alarmed, giving rise to another common name, Whistle Pigs. The American Pika (pg. 179) and Golden-mantled Ground Squirrel (pg. 125) also respond to these alarms.

The male tends to be larger than the female, having a broader head and larger body. A male will defend a territory of up to 1 acre (.4 ha) from other male marmots.

Hibernates during winter. Adults start hibernation in August, with hibernation lasting for possibly 4-7 months, depending on elevation. Mating takes place in the first few weeks after emerging from hibernation. Females do not breed until their third spring.

Some marmots are solitary. Most live in small colonies consisting of a dominant male, several females and their offspring. Young will play together while adults interact with one another, playing, sniffing, chasing each other and performing mutual grooming.

Northern

Plains

Plains
Northern
Both

Plains Pocket Gopher
Northern Pocket Gopher
Geomys bursarius and Thomomys talpoides

Family: Pocket Gophers (Geomyidae)

Size: L 7-10" (18-25 cm); Plains T 2-4" (5-10 cm), Northern T 1-3" (2.5-7.5 cm)

Weight: Plains 4½-12½ oz. (128-354 g)
Northern 2¾-4½ oz. (78-128 g)

Description: Light brown-to-gray upper. Short legs. Pink feet. Extremely long front claws. Small round ears. Tiny eyes. Short naked tail. Fur of the Northern is occasionally yellowish brown.

Origin/Age: native; 2-5 years

Compare: Other gophers (pp. 176-177) are similar in size. Wyoming Ground Squirrel (pg. 133) has a fuzzy tail. Thirteen-lined Ground Squirrel (pg. 121) has stripes along its back. Look for the large front claws and short legs to help identify the gophers.

Habitat: loose sandy soils, fields, prairies, meadows, road-side ditches, golf courses, cemeteries, pastures, Plains seen at elevations below 5,000' (1,525 m), Northern found above 5,000' (1,525 m)

Home: network of tunnels, usually with 2 levels, some about 6" (15 cm) deep, used for gathering food, deeper tunnels down to 6' (1.8 m) are used for nesting and raising young

Food: herbivore; roots, bulbs, rhizomes

Sounds: inconsequential; rarely, if ever, heard

Breeding: spring mating; 50-55 days gestation

Young: 2-6 offspring once per year; born naked and helpless with eyes closed

173

tunneling

dirt mounds

claws

Plains

Signs: mounds of excess dirt as wide as 2' (61 cm) resulting from tunneling, ridges of dirt pushed up from tunneling; opening to tunnel system only rarely seen (would require digging into a dirt mound)

Activity: diurnal, nocturnal; active year-round, alternates several hours of activity with several hours of sleep

Tracks: forepaw ⅞" (2.3 cm) long, hind paw slightly smaller, both with well-defined claw marks; spends almost all of its time in its underground tunnel system, so tracks are rarely seen

Stan's Notes: There are 35 gopher species, all unique to North America. Plains and Northern Pocket Gophers were previously thought to be a single species with only slight differences; current studies indicate they are separate species.

Specialized fur-lined cheek pouches or "pockets" give the pocket gopher its common name. This animal can stuff large amounts of food or nesting material in its pouches, which extend from the cheeks to front shoulders. Cleans the pouches by turning them inside out.

Digs with its powerful front legs and long sharp claws, preferring loose sandy soils. Specialized lips close behind its large incisor teeth, keeping dirt out of the mouth while it digs. Incisor teeth are coated with enamel and grow throughout its life. Must gnaw on hard objects to keep its teeth sharp and prevent them from growing too large and rendering them useless. Sensitive hairs and bristles (vibrissae) on the wrists and tip of tail help it feel its way through tunnels. A narrow pelvis enables it to turn around while in tunnels. Its fur can lay forward or backward and allows the animal to back up without slowing down. Has a good sense of smell, but poor hearing and eyesight.

Lives entirely underground. Feeds on roots and bulbs of different plant species, depending upon the season and availability, and stores some food in underground chambers. Has been known to pull entire plants underground by the roots. Solitary except to mate, with only one animal living in a set of tunnels and mounds.

Has adapted well to human activity, often taking up residence in open grassy yards. This animal is very beneficial to the land since its digging aerates the soil, which allows for better drainage and nutrient mixing. However, it can be destructive to gardens and fields because it eats many of the plants.

Similar species on next page   175

The word "gopher" is frequently used to describe a wide range of burrowing rodents that includes chipmunks and ground squirrels, but the term is properly restricted to pocket gophers, all of which have fur-lined cheek pouches on either side of the mouth.

Botta's Pocket Gopher occurs only in scattered locations in the southern half of Colorado. The Yellow-faced Pocket Gopher is restricted to the southeastern corner of the state. The range of the Plains and Northern Pocket Gophers covers the rest of Colorado with gophers.

Botta's Pocket Gopher 5-7"

Yellow-faced Pocket Gopher 6-8¼"

American Pika
Ochotona princeps

Family: Pikas (Ochotonidae)

Size: L 6-8½" (15-22 cm); no visible tail

Weight: 3¾-5 oz. (106-142 g)

Description: Overall brown to gray with a plump round body, short round ears and no visible tail. Hind legs are slightly longer than fore legs, allowing for running action, not hopping. Well-furred soles of feet.

Origin/Age: native; 2-3 years

Compare: Mountain Cottontail (pg. 183) is much larger and has long ears. Look for a small round critter moving quickly between and over rocks to help identify the American Pika.

Habitat: mountain talus fields, hillsides with scattered rocks, elevations from 8,000-13,500' (2,440-4,115 m)

Home: nest chamber underground or under large rocks in a protected area, lined with fine plant material

Food: herbivore; over 30 species of green plants

Sounds: muffled bleat repeated several times, shrill nasal bleats, barking and chattering teeth; gives a number of different vocalizations that seem to vary from region to region, most sounds are in response to territorial boundaries

Breeding: Apr-Jun mating; 28-30 days gestation

Young: 1-4 offspring 1-2 times per year; born blind, naked and helpless; mother cares for young, but will also go out to forage for up to a couple hours

carrying food

grooming

Signs: small to large piles of evenly cut grass and other plants laid out to dry under a rock ledge; small, round, sticky black pellets

Activity: diurnal; active all year in the morning and afternoon, may be seen sunning on a rock during winter

Tracks: hind paw 1¼-1½" (3-4 cm) long, forepaw 1-1¼" (2.5-3 cm) long, small and round; 1 set of 4 tracks

Stan's Notes: The American Pika is in the same order as rabbits and hares (Lagomorpha), but is not a rabbit or a hare. Looks only superficially like a tiny rabbit due to its extremely short ears, and forages for food in a completely different manner than rabbits.

Worldwide there are 26 pika species, most occurring in Eurasia, with two in North America. The Collared Pika (not shown) resides in Alaska and northwestern Canada. Nearly 500 miles (805 km) separates Collared populations from American Pikas, which are found in the western United States.

Unlike rabbits and hares, the pika is highly vocal, active during the day and lives in loose social groups. It maintains territories, usually running among the rocks, stopping frequently and sitting motionless for short periods to observe its domain and listen for neighboring pikas. Also known as Rock Rabbit, Whistling Hare, Cony Hare or Chief Hare. All of these names are obviously not accurate since the pika is neither a rabbit or a hare.

Feeds on up to 30 different kinds of green plants, which meet its nutritional needs. Gathers and stores food for winter. Cuts grasses and other vegetation, carries large mouthfuls to areas near its den entrance and spreads them out to dry in the sun. These piles, which often become large, are known as haystacks. Haystacks are moved frequently to facilitate drying and shelter the food from rain. Only after the greens are completely dried will they be brought into the den for later use in winter. Some speculate the pika does not actually need haystacks, but uses them as insurance for winter, should deep snow prevent access to grass.

Some studies show this species to be dying out in the southern part of its range due to climate warming. Pikas cannot travel long distances, which means populations stranded on mountain peaks eventually may die out completely.

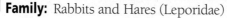

Mountain Cottontail
Sylvilagus nuttallii

Family: Rabbits and Hares (Leporidae)

Size: L 11½-12½" (29-32 cm); T 1-2" (2.5-5 cm)

Weight: 1½-2½ lb. (.7-1.1 kg)

Description: Overall gray to light brown with the center back darker than the sides. Black-tipped hairs give a salt-and-pepper appearance. White underside. Large pointed ears, the width of head, slightly furred, with a black outside edge. Rusty red nape. Brown tail with a white cotton-like underside.

Origin/Age: native; 1-3 years

Compare: Since cottontails are so similar, use range to help identify. The Desert Cottontail (pg. 187) occurs in eastern Colorado below 6,500' (1,980 m). The Eastern Cottontail (pg. 191) is in northeastern Colorado below 6,500' (1,980 m).

Habitat: mountain valleys, coniferous subalpine forests, rock piles, shrublands, thickets, elevations from 6,000-11,000' (1,830-3,355 m)

Home: shallow nest, lined with soft plant material and fur, covered with dry grasses and leaves

Food: herbivore; grass and other green plants in spring and summer; sage, saplings, twigs, bark and other woody plants in winter

Sounds: loud high-pitched scream or squeal when caught by a predator such as a fox or coyote

Breeding: late Feb-Jul mating; 28-30 days gestation; starts to breed at 8 months

Young: 3-6 offspring 3-4 times per year; born naked and helpless with eyes closed

Signs: small woody twigs and branches near the ground are cleanly cut off and at an angle, while browse from deer and elk is higher up and has a ragged edge (due to lack of upper incisors in deer and elk), bark is stripped off saplings and shrubs at the level of snow; pea-sized, round, dry, woody, light brown pellets

Activity: nocturnal, crepuscular; active year-round, often active during midday, stays in burrow for several days during inclement weather in winter

Tracks: hind paw 3-4" (7.5-10 cm) long, forepaw 1" (2.5 cm) long, small and round; 1 set of 4 tracks; forepaws fall one in front of the other behind hind prints

Stan's Notes: This is a rabbit species of areas above 6,000 feet (1,830 m), seen in the intermountain western half of the state. Tends to stay away from densely vegetated areas and wetlands.

Common name comes from the mountainous habitat where it is found and its cotton ball-like tail. Given the species name *nuttallii* and also called Nuttall's Cottontail after the early naturalist, Thomas Nuttall (1786-1859).

Active all year. Tends to be more active during the day than the other cottontail species. Often seen feeding during the middle of the day. Uses the burrows of other animals in winter, where it will hole up for a few days during bad weather. Cools itself on hot summer days, stretching out in shady areas.

Can run up to 15 mph (24 km/h) for short distances, which enables it to evade some predators. Makes a short dash when alarmed, stops and crouches, often facing away from the danger. Uses a set of well-worn trails during winter, usually under a thick cover of bushes.

Doesn't interbreed with the Desert Cottontail (pg. 187) or Eastern Cottontail (pg. 191), even where habitats overlap. Stops breeding in extreme drought conditions, reducing the competition for food and the nutritional requirements for females that otherwise would have been nursing.

Mothers nurse their babies at dawn and dusk, but may stay away for up to 24 hours at a time. Once the young open their eyes and are moving around outside the nest, they are on their own and get no further help from their mother.

Desert Cottontail

Sylvilagus audubonii

Family: Rabbits and Hares (Leporidae)

Size: L 12-13½" (30-34.5 cm); T 1-2" (2.5-5 cm)

Weight: 1¾-3 lb. (.8-1.4 kg)

Description: Overall gray to light brown with the center of the back darker than the sides. Longer black-tipped hairs, giving a grizzled appearance. Large hairless ears, longer than the length of head, with a black outside edge. Distinctive rusty red nape. Brown tail with a white cotton-like underside.

Origin/Age: native; 1-3 years

Compare: Since cottontails are so similar, use range to help identify. The Mountain Cottontail (pg. 183) is in western Colorado above 6,000' (1,830 m). The Eastern Cottontail (pg. 191) is in northeastern Colorado below 6,500' (1,980 m).

Habitat: wide variety such as open fields, brush or rock piles, along streams, shrublands, semideserts, thickets, elevations below 6,500' (1,980 m)

Home: shallow nest, lined with soft plant material and fur, covered with dry grasses and leaves

Food: herbivore; grass, dandelions, other green plants in spring and summer; raspberries, roses, saplings, twigs, bark and other woody plants in winter

Sounds: loud high-pitched scream or squeal when caught by a predator such as a fox or coyote

Breeding: year-round mating; 28 days gestation; starts to breed at 3 months

Young: 3-6 offspring 3-5 times per year; born naked and helpless with eyes closed

187

Signs: small woody twigs and branches near the ground are cleanly cut off and at an angle, while browse from deer and elk is higher up and has a ragged edge (due to lack of upper incisors in deer and elk), bark is stripped off saplings and shrubs at the level of snow; pea-sized, round, dry, woody, light brown pellets

Activity: nocturnal, crepuscular; often very active during late winter and early spring when males fight to breed with females

Tracks: hind paw 3-4" (7.5-10 cm) long, forepaw 1" (2.5 cm) long, small and round; 1 set of 4 tracks; forepaws fall one in front of the other behind hind prints

Stan's Notes: The most widespread of western cottontail species from Montana to Texas and California. Found in elevations below 6,500 feet (1,980 m) in eastern and western Colorado. Not seen in the central mountains in the state. Common name comes from the semidesert-like habitat where it is found and its cotton ball-like tail.

Usually freezes, hunkers down and flattens ears if danger is near. Able to leap up to 12-15 feet (3.7-4.5 m) in a single bound while running, jumping sideways while running to break its scent trail. Can run as fast as 15 mph (24 km/h) for a short distance, which enables it to elude some predators. Uses a well-worn set of trails in winter, usually under thick cover of bushes. When flushed, it runs quickly in a zigzag pattern, circling back to its starting spot. On hot, lazy summer days, it will stretch out in shady areas to cool itself.

Males often remain in a small area of only 10-15 acres (4-6 ha), while females reside in areas about half that size. Usually not a territorial animal, but fights will break out among males during mating season. Interspersed with chasing, males face each other, kick with front feet and jump high into the air.

After mating, the female excavates a small area for a nest, lines it with soft plants and fur from her chest for comfort and camouflages the entrance. Mothers nurse their babies at dawn and dusk, but may stay away for up to a day at a time. Once the young open their eyes and are moving around outside the nest, they are on their own and no longer receive help from their mother.

A successful rabbit species, with females usually breeding before they reach 1 year of age and some producing up to 35 offspring annually. Most of the cottontail young, however, do not live any longer than a year.

Eastern Cottontail
Sylvilagus floridanus

Family: Rabbits and Hares (Leporidae)

Size: L 14-18" (36-45 cm); T 1-2" (2.5-5 cm)

Weight: 2-4 lb. (.9-1.8 kg)

Description: Overall gray to light brown. Black-tipped hairs give it a grizzled appearance. Usually has a small white (rarely black) spot on forehead between the ears. Large pointed ears, rarely with a black outside edge. Distinctive rusty red nape. Brown tail with a white cotton-like underside.

Origin/Age: native; 1-3 years

Compare: Since cottontails are so similar, use range to help identify. Desert Cottontail (pg. 187) is smaller and much more widespread in Colorado. Mountain Cottontail (pg. 183) occurs in the western half of the state in elevations above 6,000' (1,830 m).

Habitat: wide variety such as open fields, brush piles, rock piles, along rivers and streams, woodlands, thickets, elevations below 6,500' (1,980 m)

Home: shallow nest, lined with soft plant material and fur, covered with dry grasses and leaves

Food: herbivore; grass, dandelions, other green plants in spring and summer; raspberries, roses, saplings, twigs, bark and other woody plants in winter

Sounds: loud high-pitched scream or squeal when caught by a predator such as a fox or coyote

Breeding: late Feb-Mar mating; 30 days gestation; starts to breed at 3 months

Young: 3-6 offspring up to 5 times per year; born naked and helpless with eyes closed

191

camouflaged

scat

Signs: small woody twigs and branches near the ground are cleanly cut off and at an angle, while browse from deer is higher up and has a ragged edge (due to the lack of upper incisors in deer), bark is stripped off of saplings and shrubs at the level of snow; dry, pea-sized light brown pellets, round and woody; soft green pellets are ingested and rarely seen

Activity: nocturnal, crepuscular; often very active during late winter and early spring when males fight to breed with females

Tracks: hind paw 3-4" (7.5-10 cm) long, forepaw 1" (2.5 cm) long, small and round; 1 set of 4 tracks; forepaws fall one in front of the other behind hind prints

Stan's Notes: The most widespread of the eight cottontail species in North America, seen in the eastern United States and most of Mexico, but found only in a small part of Colorado's northeastern plains. Transplanted to many areas that historically did not have cottontails. Common name comes from its cotton ball-like tail.

Usually stays in a small area of only a couple acres. Often freezes, hunkers down and flattens ears if danger is near. Quickly runs in a zigzag pattern, circling back to its starting spot when flushed. Able to leap up to 12-15 feet (3.7-4.5 m) in a single bound while running. Also jumps sideways while running to break its scent trail. Uses a set of well-worn trails in winter, usually in thick cover of bushes. Cools itself on hot summer days by stretching out in shaded grassy areas.

Usually not a territorial animal, with fights among males breaking out only during mating season. Interspersed with chasing, males face each other, kick with front feet and jump high into the air.

After mating, the female excavates a small area for a nest, lines it with soft plants and fur from her chest for comfort and camouflages the entrance. Mothers nurse their babies at dawn and dusk. Once the young open their eyes and are moving outside the nest, they are on their

cooling

own and get no further help from their mother. One of the most reproductively successful rabbit species in North America, with some females producing as many as 35 offspring annually; however, most young do not live longer than 1 year.

Like other rabbits and hares, this species produces fecal pellets that are dry and brown or soft and green. Eats the green pellets to regain the nutrition that wasn't digested initially.

Snowshoe Hare

Lepus americanus

Family: Rabbits and Hares (Leporidae)

Size: L 15-20" (38-50 cm); T 1-2" (2.5-5 cm)

Weight: 2-3 lb. (.9-1.4 kg)

Description: Overall rusty brown during summer with black-tipped hair, giving it a dark grizzled appearance. Large well-furred hind feet with white "stockings." Long pointed ears, black along edges. Dark brown eyes. Belly is light gray to white. Tail is brown above, gray or white below. All white in winter with a brown nose and black-tipped ears.

Origin/Age: native; 2-3 years

Compare: Very similar to Mountain Cottontail (pg. 183) during summer, which is smaller and lacks the white hind feet. During winter the all-white coat and black-tipped ears make it easy to identify.

Habitat: coniferous mountain forests, subalpine and near tundra, elevations from 7,000-12,000' (2,135-3,660 m)

Home: shallow nest in a protected area under rocks and vegetation, known as a form

Food: herbivore; green plants and fruit in summer, twigs, bark, coniferous needles and buds in winter

Sounds: inconsequential; may give a loud squeal when captured by a large predator

Breeding: Apr-Aug mating; 37-40 days gestation

Young: 1-7 offspring 2-3 times per year; born with fur and eyes open, able to run within hours of birth; mother leaves young unattended, visits a couple times each day to nurse

195

winter

Signs: well-worn trails in snow from frequent use; dry, pea-sized light brown pellets, woody and round with one side slightly flattened, slightly larger than cottontail pellets

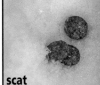

scat

Activity: mostly nocturnal; seen during short, overcast days in deep winter

Tracks: hind paw 4-5" (10-13 cm) long and 2" (5 cm) wide, forepaw 1" (2.5 cm) long, small and round; 1 set of 4 tracks; forepaws fall one in front of the other behind hind prints

Stan's Notes: Named "Snowshoe" for its large hind feet. Extra fur grows on the hind feet in winter, enabling it to move across deep, soft snow. Has brown fur in summer, white fur in winter. Between seasons it can be patchy brown and white in color, often matching its environment of partially snow-covered ground. Seasonal molts are triggered by decreasing or increasing hours of daylight.

Frequently runs in circles when chased, traveling up to 30 mph (48 km/h) and bounding up to 14 feet (4.3 m). Often heads for thick vegetation for cover. Uses the wallows of grouse to take dust baths in summer. Usually lives a solitary life except to mate.

Rarely ventures into open areas, preferring to stay under or near some vegetative cover. Unless flushed, it remains hunkered down during the day, leaving on well-traveled paths at night to feed.

Populations go up and down in 10-year cycles. The causes of these fluctuations are not well understood, but most likely are tied to the abundance of food and populations of predators such as goshawks and coyotes.

Hunted by all sorts of predators, making it a very important part of the ecosystem. Only an estimated 15-20 percent of juveniles make it to adulthood. Survival rate for Snowshoe adults is only 45 percent.

Black-tailed Jackrabbit
Lepus californicus

Family: Rabbits and Hares (Leporidae)

Size: L 18-24" (45-61 cm); T 2-3" (5-7.5 cm)

Weight: 4-8 lb. (1.8-3.6 kg)

Description: Gray to light brown in summer with black-tipped hair, giving it a grizzled appearance. Light white belly. Extremely long, black-tipped ears. Long legs. Large hind feet. Large brown eyes. A large, puffy white tail with black on top and extending onto the rump. All white in winter, sometimes with brown patches. Black-tipped white ears.

Origin/Age: native; 1-5 years

Compare: The White-tailed Jackrabbit (pg. 203) is slightly larger and lacks black on the tail or back. The Snowshoe Hare (pg. 195) also turns white in winter, but is much smaller and has shorter ears.

Habitat: semideserts, scrublands, grasslands, elevations below 7,000' (2,135 m)

Home: shallow nest under sagebrush and other shrubs or beneath logs, lined with dry grasses and hair from the mother, uses a burrow in winter

Food: herbivore; green plants in summer, twigs, bark, leaf buds, dried grasses and berries in winter

Sounds: inconsequential; may give a loud, shrill scream when captured by a large predator

Breeding: Feb-May mating; 30-40 days gestation

Young: 1-11 offspring 4-5 times per year; born fully furred with eyes open and incisor teeth erupted, able to move around within an hour of birth

199

Signs: trails worn between feeding areas and resting sites, deep snow on trails in winter packed down from frequent use; hard, dry, woody, slightly flattened, dark brown pellets, ½" (1 cm) wide, or moist green pellets

Activity: mostly nocturnal, crepuscular; can be seen during cloudy or overcast days

Tracks: hind paw 4-5½" (10-14 cm) long and 2" (5 cm) wide, forepaw 1" (2.5 cm) long, small and round; 1 set of 4 tracks; forepaws are slightly offset side by side or fall one in front of the other behind hind prints

Stan's Notes: The most abundant jackrabbit across most of the western states including Colorado. Seen mostly in the eastern half of the state in areas below 7,000 feet (2,135 m). Viewed as competition for rangelands and widely hunted by organized hunting parties in the late 1800s.

Sometimes called Jackass Rabbit, although it is actually a type of hare. Hard to misidentify since it is so large and runs with a see-saw-like rocking from front to hind feet. Black on tail and rump is best seen when it runs. Can leap as far as 20 feet (6.1 m) and run up to 45 mph (72 km/h) for a short distance, slowing to a series of low leaps from 4-10 feet (1.2-3 m).

The enormous ears have a generous blood flow, which dissipates heat during summer. The ears also provide an excellent means of predator detection. The large hind legs facilitate high jumps and quick escapes from predators and are used for defense, kicking and scratching with its claws. Does not like water, but is a good swimmer and may plunge into water to escape a predator.

Usually solitary, but may be seen in large groups, especially in spring when it gathers for mating. Females can be slightly larger than males (bucks), but there are no obvious differences between sexes. When bucks fight, they kick with hind feet and bite.

Rests under logs or other shelter (shade) during the day and will flush only if contact is very close. In winter it snuggles in burrows or snow caves that may be connected by tunnels, resting with its large ears pressed flat against its back.

Female constructs a simple nest—a shallow depression lined with grasses and fur plucked from her chest. Babies can run within an hour of their birth. They are eating plants at 2 weeks and weaned shortly after, fully independent at 4 weeks. If born early enough in the season, young females can breed before their first winter.

Reingestion of soft fecal pellets (coprophagy) occurs in hares, as it does in rabbits.

White-tailed Jackrabbit
Lepus townsendii

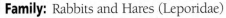

Family: Rabbits and Hares (Leporidae)

Size: L 22-26" (56-66 cm); T 3-4" (7.5-10 cm)

Weight: 5-9 lb. (2.3-4.1 kg)

Description: Gray to light brown in summer with black-tipped hair, giving it a grizzled appearance. Light gray belly. Extremely long, black-tipped ears. Long legs. Large hind feet. Large brown eyes. A large, puffy white tail. All white in winter, sometimes with brown patches. Black-tipped white ears.

Origin/Age: native; 1-5 years

Compare: The Black-tailed Jackrabbit (pg. 199) is slightly smaller and has black on the upper surface of its tail extending to the center of its back. Snowshoe Hare (pg. 195) also turns white in winter, but is smaller than White-tailed and has shorter ears.

Habitat: open mountain valleys, alpine tundra, scrublands, semideserts, elevations from 4,000-14,000' (1,220-4,270 m)

Home: shallow nest in grassy open areas or under logs, lined with dry grasses and hair from the mother, may not make a nest, uses a burrow in winter

Food: herbivore, green plants in summer, twigs, bark, leaf buds, dried grasses and berries in winter

Sounds: inconsequential; may give a loud, shrill scream when captured by a large predator

Breeding: Mar-Aug mating; 30-40 days gestation

Young: 1-11 offspring 1-2 times per year; born fully furred with eyes open and incisor teeth erupted, able to move around within an hour of birth

winter

Signs: deep snow on trails in winter packed down from frequent use; hard, dry, woody, light brown pellets or soft, moist green pellets

scat

Activity: mostly nocturnal, crepuscular; can be seen during cloudy or overcast days

Tracks: hind paw 5-6" (13-15 cm) long and 2-2½" (5-6 cm) wide, forepaw 1" (2.5 cm) long, small and round; 1 set of 4 tracks; forepaws are slightly offset side by side or fall one in front of the other behind hind prints

Stan's Notes: Widely distributed throughout Colorado except for the extreme southwestern and southeastern corners of the state. Closely related to the Black-tailed Jackrabbit (pg. 199), which occurs in sagebrush habitat below 7,000 feet (2,135 m). By far the largest of rabbit-like animals in the state, it is actually a type of hare. Hard to misidentify because it is so large and runs with a seesaw like rocking back and forth from front to hind feet. Able to leap up to 20 feet (6.1 m) and run as fast as 45 mph (72 km/h) for short distances, then slows to a series of low leaps ranging from 4-10 feet (1.2-3 m).

The enormous ears have a generous blood flow, which dissipates heat during summer. The ears also provide an excellent means of predator detection. The large hind legs facilitate high jumps and quick escapes from predators and are used in defense, kicking and scratching with its claws.

Often solitary but can be seen in large groups, especially in spring when it gathers for mating. Females can be slightly larger than males (bucks), but there are no obvious differences between the sexes. Bucks fight by kicking with hind feet and biting.

Rests under logs or some kind of shelter (shade) during the day and will flush only if contact is extremely close. During winter it snuggles in burrows or snow caves that may be connected by tunnels, resting with its large ears pressed flat against its back. Does not like water, but is a good swimmer and may plunge into water to escape a predator.

Female builds a simple nest consisting of a shallow depression lined with grasses and fur she has plucked from her chest. Babies can run within an hour of birth. They are eating plants at 2 weeks and weaned shortly after, fully independent at 4 weeks.

Reingestion of soft fecal pellets (coprophagy) occurs in hares, as it does in rabbits.

winter

Short-tailed Weasel
Mustela erminea

Family: Weasels and Skunks (Mustelidae)

Size: L 7-10" (18-25 cm); T 2-4" (5-10 cm)

Weight: 2-6 oz. (57-170 g)

Description: Light to dark brown with a black-tipped brown tail and white chin, throat, chest, belly and feet in summer. Long, thin tubular body. Short legs. White in winter with a black-tipped tail. Male is slightly larger than female.

Origin/Age: native; 3-7 years

Compare: Smaller than Mink (pg. 219), which has a white patch on the chin and lacks a white throat, chest and belly. Long-tailed Weasel (pg. 211) is also all white in winter with a black-tipped tail, but has a white-to-yellow underside in summer.

Habitat: open mixed forests, wetlands, prairies, elevations above 6,000' (1,830 m)

Home: burrow, often an old chipmunk burrow; several burrows scattered in its territory

Food: carnivore, insectivore; small to medium animals such as mice, voles, chipmunks, rabbits and Pine Squirrels (pg. 145); also eats insects

Sounds: loud chatters, piercing shrills, hisses if threatened

Breeding: summer (July) mating; 27-28 days gestation; implantation is delayed up to 8-9 months after mating

Young: 4-9 offspring once per year

changing color

scat

Signs: long thin scat with a pointed end, often contains hair and bones

Activity: primarily nocturnal, diurnal mostly in winter; hunts during the day for several hours, then rests and sleeps for several hours

Tracks: hind paw ¾-1" (2-2.5 cm) long, forepaw slightly smaller, both round with well-defined nail marks, 5 toes on all feet; 1 set of 4 tracks when bounding; 10-12" (25-30 cm) stride

Stan's Notes: This is a small weasel with a big attitude, capturing and killing animals several times its own weight. Chases, pounces, then kills its prey with one or more bites to the base of the skull, severing the spinal cord. Like other weasels, usually laps up blood from prey before eating it, giving rise to the myth that the weasel kills just to suck the blood from its victims. Occasionally catches and kills more than it can eat and caches the extra food.

Always on the move, hunting mostly on the ground, but can climb trees. Excellent sight and smell. Rarely seen more than one at a time except when the female is teaching her offspring to hunt.

winter

Male has a larger territory than the female. Matures sexually in the second year. Male drags the female around by the scruff of the neck during mating, which may last several hours. Males mating with mothers that have offspring may also mate with their female young.

Female matures sexually the summer of her first year. Usually the female raises the young by herself, but there are some reports of the male helping. Offspring are taught to hunt by 6-10 weeks.

Also known as Stoat during summer, when the animal is brown. Like the Long-tailed Weasel (pg. 211), it is referred to as Ermine during winter, when it is all white except for the black-tipped tail.

Long-tailed Weasel
Mustela frenata

Family: Weasels and Skunks (Mustelidae)

Size: L 8-16" (20-40 cm); T 3-6" (7.5-15 cm)

Weight: 3-9 oz. (85-255 g)

Description: Light brown in summer with a long black-tipped brown tail, brown feet and white-to-yellow chin, throat, chest and belly. Long tubular body. Short legs. White in the winter with a black-tipped tail. Male slightly larger than female.

Origin/Age: native; 5-10 years

Compare: Larger than Short-tailed Weasel (pg. 207), which has a shorter tail and white feet. Mink (pg. 219) is larger, darker brown with a white patch on the chin and doesn't turn white during winter.

Habitat: forests, fields, wetlands, prairies, farms, elevations from 6,000-12,000' (1,830-3,660 m)

Home: nest made from grass and fur, usually in an old chipmunk, ground squirrel or mole burrow or under logs and rocks; often has several nests in its territory

Food: carnivore, insectivore; small to medium mammals such as voles, mice, chipmunks, squirrels and rabbits; will also eat small birds, bird eggs, carrion and insects

Sounds: single loud trills or rapid trills, squeals

Breeding: summer (Jul-Aug) mating; 30-34 days gestation; ova develop for 8 days after fertilization, then cease development, implantation is delayed up to 8-10 months after mating

Young: 4-8 offspring once per year from April to June

Signs: long, thin, often dark scat with a pointed end, contains hair and bones, often on a log or rock, very similar to mink scat

Activity: primarily nocturnal, diurnal mostly during the winter; hunts during the day for several hours, then rests and sleeps for several hours

Tracks: hind paw ¾-1" (2-2.5 cm) long, forepaw slightly smaller, both round with well-defined nail marks, 5 toes on all feet; 1 set of 4 tracks when bounding; 12-20" (30-50 cm) stride

Stan's Notes: This is a very active predator that runs in a series of bounds with its back arched and tail elevated. Found mainly in the mountains up to 12,000 feet (3,660 m). Also seen in the flat eastern half of the state.

A good swimmer and will climb trees to pursue squirrels. Quickly locates prey using its excellent eyesight and sense of smell, dashes to grab it, then kills it with several bites to the base of the skull. Favorite foods include the Meadow Vole (pg. 77) and Deer Mouse (pg. 51). Usually hunts for larger prey such as rabbits. Eats its fill and caches the rest. Consumes 25-40 percent of its own body weight in food daily.

winter

Uses odor and sound to communicate with other weasels. Deposits scat onto rocks or along trails to mark territory. Male maintains a territory of 25-55 acres (10-22 ha); female territory is smaller. Both sexes apply a smelly, oily substance secreted from the anal glands onto rocks, trees and other prominent landmarks to communicate their sex, social status, territory and willingness to mate. Can be seen depositing the substance, but the odor is rarely detectible to humans, especially after a few days. Will defend territory against other weasels.

Solitary except during mating season and when a mother is with her young. Constructs nest in an abandoned animal burrow or beneath logs and rocks, using grass and the fur of small animals it has eaten for nesting material.

American Marten
Martes americana

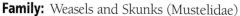

Family: Weasels and Skunks (Mustelidae)

Size: L 12-21" (30-53 cm); T 5-9" (13-22.5 cm); H 6-7" (15-18 cm)

Weight: 1-4 lb. (.5-1.8 kg)

Description: Body ranges from light brown to nearly blond or dark brown to nearly black. Head is lighter in color than the body, usually gray to nearly white. Large ears and short snout. Light orange or buff throat patch. Long bushy tail. Male slightly larger than female.

Origin/Age: native; 5-15 years

Compare: Short-tailed Weasel (pg. 207) is brown during summer and white in winter, with a black-tipped tail year-round. Mink (pg. 219) has a white patch on the chin and a thin dark-tipped tail.

Habitat: coniferous forests, wetlands, elevations above 7,000' (2,135 m)

Home: burrow, often a hollow log or tree or rock crevice, may use an old squirrel nest or woodpecker hole

Food: omnivore; small mammals such as mice, voles, squirrels, chipmunks and rabbits; also eats birds, eggs, berries, insects, earthworms and pine seeds

Sounds: snarls and hisses when threatened, various huffs and screams during mating

Breeding: midsummer mating; 26-27 days gestation; implantation is delayed up to 6-8 months after mating

Young: 2-5 (usually 2) offspring once per year in March or April; born naked with eyes closed, weaned at 5-6 weeks, nearly adult size at about 90 days

Signs: small, dark and often thin scat, usually containing hair and bones, seen at scat stations where droppings are repeatedly deposited, used to mark territory, closely resembles mink scat

Activity: diurnal, nocturnal; active year-round, especially on overcast days

Tracks: hind paw 1½-1¾" (4-4.5 cm) long, forepaw slightly smaller; 1 set of 4 tracks when bounding; 6-8" (15-20 cm) stride, sometimes has a tail drag mark; tracks may be seen in snow, often leading to and from trees

Stan's Notes: Solitary, inquisitive and an excellent tree climber. Also known as Pine Marten because of its close association with coniferous forests. Its thick fur is well suited for life in a snowy environment and high elevations. A strong swimmer, even underwater. Like other weasels, it often has a musky odor. Very vocal when encountering another marten, snarling and baring its teeth.

Diet consists of more than 100 types of food, nearly all of it meat. Prefers Pine Squirrels (pg. 145) and Fox Squirrels (pg. 153), often taking over their nests after killing and eating them. Looks much like a squirrel when searching on the ground for voles.

The male has a home range of 5-15 square miles (13-39 sq. km). Female range is smaller.

Much play and wrestling during courtship, which lasts as long as a couple weeks. Breeds with several mates (polygamous) each season.

Female matures sexually at 15 months and scent marks to advertise she is receptive to mating. Mother marten often leaves her young after weaning them, and mates again.

Habitat destruction and trapping has led to a sharp decrease in the population over the past century. Some people have attracted martens to their yards by setting out raw chicken or other meats. This is not recommended.

Mink
Neovison vison

Family: Weasels and Skunks (Mustelidae)

Size: L 14-20" (36-50 cm); T 6-8" (15-20 cm)

Weight: 1½-3½ lb. (.7-1.6 kg)

Description: Dark brown to nearly black or brown to blond, often with a luster. Short, round dark ears. Small white patch on the chin. Long tubular body with short legs. A long bushy tail, darker near the tip. Male slightly larger than female.

Origin/Age: native; 5-10 years

Compare: Larger than Long-tailed Weasel (pg. 211), which is lighter brown with white-to-yellow underside. Much larger than Short-tailed Weasel (pg. 207), which has a shorter tail and white underside. Mink does not turn white in winter.

Habitat: along rivers, lakes and streams, wetlands, farms, forests, all elevations throughout Colorado

Home: burrow, entrance is 4" (10 cm) wide

Food: carnivore; small to medium mammals such as voles, mice, chipmunks, rabbits and squirrels, but favors muskrats; also eats small birds, bird eggs, snakes, frogs, toads, crayfish and fish

Sounds: chatters, scolds, hisses, snarls when alarmed or fighting other minks

Breeding: Jan-Apr mating; 32-51 days gestation; implantation delayed, length of delay is dependent upon when the female mates during the season

Young: 3-6 offspring once per year; born covered with fine hair and eyes closed, eyes open at about 7 weeks, weaned at 8-9 weeks, mature at 5 months

brown morph

scat

Signs: small, thin dark scat, usually pointed at one end, usually containing bone, fur and fish scales, deposited on rocks and logs along lakes and rivers

Activity: nocturnal, diurnal; hunts for several hours, then rests several hours

Tracks: hind paw 2-3¼" (5-8 cm) long with 5 toes, forepaw 1¼-1¾" (3-4.5 cm) long with 5 toes, both round with well-defined nail marks; 1 set of 4 tracks when bounding; 12-25" (30-64 cm) stride; tracks may end at the edge of water

Stan's Notes: Also known as the American Mink. Usually seen along the banks of rivers and lakes all across the northern half of Colorado from prairies to high mountains. Its thick, oily, water-proof fur provides great insulation and enables the animal to swim in nearly freezing water. Its partially webbed toes aid in swimming. Can swim as far as 100 feet (30 m) underwater before surfacing. Able to dive down to 15 feet (4.5 m) for one of its favorite foods, muskrats.

Hunts on land for chipmunks, rabbits, snakes and frogs. Moves in a series of loping bounds with its back arched and tail held out slightly above horizontal. When frightened or excited, releases an odorous substance from glands near the base of its tail.

Burrow is almost always near water, often under a tree root or in a riverbank. May use a hollow log or muskrat burrow after killing and eating the occupants. Active burrows will often have a strong odor near the entrance. Most burrows are temporary since minks are almost constantly on the move looking for their next meal.

The male maintains a territory of up to 40 acres (16 ha), with the female territory less than half the size. Will mark its territory by applying a pungent discharge on prominent rocks and logs. It is a polygamous breeder.

The pelt of a mink is considered to be one of the most luxurious. Demand for the fur has led to the establishment of mink ranches, where the fur color can be controlled by selective breeding.

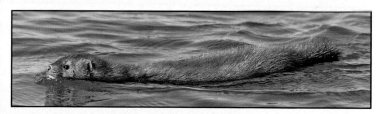

RARE

Black-footed Ferret
Mustela nigripes

Family: Weasels and Skunks (Mustelidae)

Size: L 15½-19" (39-48 cm); T 4-5½" (10-14 cm)

Weight: 1½-2¼ lb. (.7-1 kg)

Description: Body is tan to yellowish brown with a dark stripe down the center of back. Black mask around eyes. Elongated tubular body with short legs. Black legs and feet. Light-colored tail with a black tip.

Origin/Age: native; 5-10 years

Compare: Larger and much lighter in color than the Mink (pg. 219), which is usually dark brown to nearly black. Larger than Long-tailed Weasel (pg. 211) and Short-tailed Weasel (pg. 207), both of which lack the black mask, legs and feet of the Ferret.

Habitat: prairies, fields, prairie dog towns

Home: takes over a prairie dog burrow or ground squirrel tunnel; home range of 20-50 acres (8-20 ha) or more

Food: carnivore; mainly prairie dogs; also eats ground squirrels, rabbits, reptiles and some insects

Sounds: much growling and snarling when cornered

Breeding: winter (Feb-Mar) mating; 42-45 days gestation; no delayed implantation

Young: 3-5 offspring once per year in April or May; first appears aboveground in July, when it is about three-quarters the size of an adult

Signs: narrow piles of freshly excavated dirt at the entrance of a burrow; long, thin, often dark scat with a pointed end, contains hair and bones, very similar to mink scat

Activity: primarily nocturnal, diurnal only during winter when adults are looking for mates and moving from burrow to burrow during the day; most active between one and four o'clock in the morning during the rest of the year, hunts mainly at night until it catches something, then rests for up to 6 days, feeding on its kill

Tracks: hind paw 2-2¾" (5-7 cm) long, forepaw slightly smaller, both round with well-defined nail marks, 5 toes on all feet; 1 set of 4 tracks when bounding; 12-20" (30-50 cm) stride

Stan's Notes: The least known of all weasels in North America. Was listed as an endangered species prior to being declared extinct in 1979, when the last ferret died in a zoo. No wild ferrets were known to exist, but in 1981, a ranch dog in Meeteetse, Wyoming, brought home the body of a Black-footed Ferret, which led to the discovery of a small wild population. By 1985 the wild population was struck with a fatal disease, killing all but 18 individuals. These few remaining ferrets were trapped and bred in captivity. Starting in 1991, the ferrets were reintroduced back to the wild in several states including Colorado, where they are now holding their own.

Black-footed Ferrets have coevolved with prairie dogs and are so closely linked, you can't find ferrets without a prairie dog town. Ferrets use prairie dog burrows for their homes and hunt and eat prairie dogs for food. A ferret might expand the burrow or add chambers and will often leave the burrow and take up residency in another one as it searches for food.

Ferrets live alone in burrows and will come together only during mating or when females have young. Young leave their mothers at the end of their first summer and are sexually mature at 1 year of age. Will start to breed right away and may live up to 10 years in the wild. Extremely nocturnal, only coming aboveground well after dark, and usually back in the burrow well before daylight.

Very susceptible to canine distemper, resulting in many ferret deaths. Also suffers from plague. Highly impacted by poisoning programs designed to control prairie dogs.

Prospects for the survival of the Black-footed Ferret are good as long as the prairie dog population stays healthy and the habitat remains intact.

American Badger

Taxidea taxus

Family: Weasels and Skunks (Mustelidae)

Size: L 20-30" (50-76 cm); T 3-6" (7.5-15 cm)

Weight: 8-25 lb. (3.6-11.3 kg)

Description: Coarse, grizzled gray upper and yellowish brown underside. A dark snout with a distinctive white stripe from the nose upward, between the eyes and to the nape. White cheeks and ears. Large wide body. Short powerful legs with long, sharp nonretractable (nonretractile) nails on front feet. Small gray tail. Male larger than female.

Origin/Age: native; 3-10 years

Compare: Wolverine (pg. 231) is darker brown. Badger has shorter legs and its body is closer to the ground.

Habitat: along roads, fields, prairies, woodland edges, all elevations

Home: large den, often in a road embankment or grassy hillside, digs its own, may overtake and enlarge a prairie dog burrow; uses den for birthing, raising young and during torpor

Food: carnivore, insectivore; small mammals such as voles, mice, chipmunks, rabbits and ground squirrels; also eats small birds, bird eggs, snakes, frogs, toads and insects

Sounds: loud snarls and growls

Breeding: Jul-Aug mating; 30-40 days gestation; implantation delayed until February after mating

Young: 1-5 offspring once per year in March or April; born covered with fine fur and eyes closed, eyes open at about 4 weeks, weaned at about 8 weeks

227

den entrance

scat

Signs: large pile of unearthed dirt in front of den entrance, can be seen from a great distance, bones, uneaten body parts and scat frequently scattered near the den entrance; long thin scat, segmented, often dark, contains hair and bones

Activity: nocturnal; usually does not leave den until well after dark to hunt for small mammals, occasionally leaves den during the day

Tracks: forepaw and hind paw 2" (5 cm) long and wide, round with narrow pad, separate nail marks, 5 distinct toes on all feet; fore and hind prints fall near each other when walking, 6-12" (15-30 cm) stride

Stan's Notes: The least weasel-like of weasels. Uniquely shaped, its wide flattened body, short powerful legs and narrow snout make it well suited to burrow and live underground. Has second eyelids (nictitating membranes), which protect its eyes while it digs. Uses its long, sharp front claws to dig through coarse rocky soil, expelling dirt between its hind legs like a dog. Can dig fast enough to capture ground squirrels and moles while they are still in their burrows. Has an excellent sense of smell. Believed to be able to determine just by the scent of a burrow whether or not it is occupied.

Secretive and avoids contact with people. Has the reputation of being aggressive, especially a mother defending her young. Very vocal when threatened, snarling and growling loudly.

Hunts cooperatively with coyotes. While a badger excavates one tunnel entrance, a coyote will wait for the occupant to emerge at an auxiliary escape tunnel. Frequently the coyote will chase the occupant back down the burrow to the waiting badger.

It is not a true hibernator, but enters a condition called torpor that resembles hibernation, during which the body temperature falls approximately 10°F (-12°C) and heart rate and respiration decrease to approximately half the normal rate. Torpor lasts only 20-30 hours at a time. Badgers remain awake for up to 24 hours between periods of torpor, during which time body temperature and heart rate return to normal. Because of this energy-saving torpor cycle, the body rarely uses up its stored fat by spring.

Male has a large home range, where several females also may live. Lacks a family structure. Male stays solitary while female raises young on her own. Young stay with the mother until their first autumn, when they are fully grown and can hunt on their own.

Wolverine
Gulo gulo

Family: Weasels and Skunks (Mustelidae)

Size: L 25-36" (64-91 cm); T 6-10" (15-25 cm)

Weight: 18-38 lb. (8.1-17.1 kg)

Description: Dark brown with 2 yellowish brown bands along sides from shoulders to base of tail. Broad head, light brown ears, dark muzzle. Large body. Full furry tail, darker at tip. Male is 10 percent larger than female.

Origin/Age: native; 5-10 years

Compare: Larger than American Badger (pg. 227), which has distinct white markings on head and much shorter legs.

Habitat: forests, along lakes and streams, prairies, elevations above 7,500' (2,285 m)

Home: den, under a large rock or beneath the roots of a fallen tree, in a crevice or cave, female will dig a snow cave in higher elevations; used for birthing and raising young

Food: carnivore; medium to large animals such as hares, squirrels, Yellow-bellied Marmots (pg. 169), skunks, foxes, porcupines, deer; also eats carrion

Sounds: generally quiet, will snort, growl and huff when it is upset

Breeding: Apr-Aug mating; 30-40 days gestation; implantation delayed until November or December after mating

Young: 1-5 kits once every 2 years in March or April; born with eyes closed, weaned at approximately 10 weeks, stays with mother for up to a year

Signs: large, long cylindrical scat, tapered at one or both ends, often segmented, usually contains hair and bones

Activity: nocturnal, diurnal; alternates hunting and resting every 3-4 hours

Tracks: forepaw and hind paw 4-6" (10-15 cm) long, round with well-defined pad and 5 nail marks, 5 toes on all feet; alternating fore and hind prints when walking, 4-8" (10-20 cm) stride

Stan's Notes: Extremely rare in Colorado. Historically found in the central mountains of northern Colorado, where it was trapped to near extinction by the early 1900s for its rich warm fur. Since then, only a few sightings have been reported. Its range includes northern Europe and Siberia and throughout northern North America. It is one of the least-studied large mammals in North America due to its naturally low density population. Any sighting of one of these animals should be reported to the Colorado Division of Wildlife.

One of the largest members of the Weasel family. Reported to be the strongest mammal for its size. Can run with a loping gallop of about 10 mph (16 km/h). An excellent tree climber and strong swimmer. Like other weasels, it gives off a musky-smelling odor when threatened. Has an excellent sense of smell, but poor eyesight. This is a solitary animal that does not hibernate. Seems to enjoy snow and cold, living most of its life on the tundra or in high elevations where snow and ice rarely melt.

The genus and species names are the same and mean "glutton." Once called Glutton due to its misperceived voracious appetite; it simply eats what it can find, no more than any other animal of its size. Hunts mostly smaller animals, such as rabbits and ground squirrels, but able to kill animals as large as White-tailed Deer (pg. 323). While it has the reputation of a ruthless killer, it feeds mainly on winter-killed animals. Fearless, it is known for driving large predators such as bears, mountain lions and even lone wolves from their kills to scavenge the remains. Caches extra food and marks it with a musky scent, presumably to keep any other animals away.

Will wander very long distances for extended periods of time in search of food. Male has a territory of more than 200 square miles (520 sq. km); female territory is about half the size. Long mating season compensates for its sparse distribution.

Northern River Otter
Lontra canadensis

Family: Weasels and Skunks (Mustelidae)

Size: L 2½-3½' (76-107 cm); T 11-20" (28-50 cm)

Weight: 10-30 lb. (4.5-13.5 kg)

Description: Overall dark brown-to-black fur, especially when wet, with a lighter brown-to-gray belly. Silver-to-gray chin and throat. Small ears and eyes. Short snout with white whiskers. Elongated body with a long thick tail, tapered at the tip. Male slightly larger than female.

Origin/Age: native; 7-20 years

Compare: Much larger than Mink (pg. 219) and Muskrat (pg. 79). Mink has a white patch on the chin and lacks a long thick tail. Muskrat has a long, thin naked tail.

Habitat: rivers, streams, medium to large lakes, elevations up to 8,500' (2,590 m)

Home: permanent and temporary dens

Food: carnivore, insectivore; fish, crayfish, frogs, small mammals, aquatic insects

Sounds: loud shrill cries when threatened, during play will grunt, growl and snort, chuckles when with mate or siblings

Breeding: Mar-Apr mating; 200-270 days gestation; implantation delayed for an unknown amount of time, entire reproduction process may take up to 1 year, female mates again days after giving birth

Young: 1-6 offspring once per year in March or April; born fully furred with eyes closed, eyes open at around 30 days, weaned at about 3 months

235

sleeping

scat

Signs: haul outs, slides and rolling areas; scat is dark brown to green, short segments frequently contain fish bones and scales or crayfish parts, deposited on lakeshores, riverbanks, rocks or logs in water

Activity: diurnal, nocturnal; active year-round, spends most of time in water, comes onto land to rest and sleep, curls up like a house cat to sleep

Tracks: hind paw 3½" (9 cm), forepaw slightly smaller, both round with a well-defined heel pad and toes spread evenly apart, 5 toes on all feet; 1 set of 4 tracks when bounding; 12-24" (30-61 cm) stride

Stan's Notes: A large semiaquatic animal once found throughout Colorado in major bodies of water, but wiped out (extirpated) by hunting and trapping. Reintroduction began around the state in the mid-1970s to 1980s. Listed as threatened in Colorado.

Well suited to life in water, with a streamlined body, webbed toes, long guard hairs and dense oily undercoat. Special valves close the nostrils underwater, enabling submersion for up to 6-8 minutes.

A playful, social animal, not often very afraid of humans. Can be seen in small groups (mostly mothers with young), swimming and fishing in rivers and lakes. Frequently raises its head high while treading water to survey surroundings. Enjoys sliding on its belly down well-worn areas of mud, snow or ice (slides) on a riverbank or lakeshore just for fun. Can dive to depths of 50 feet (15 m). Sensitive to water pollution, quickly leaving a contaminated area.

Often feeds on slow-moving fish that are easy to catch such as catfish and suckers. Mistakenly blamed for eating too many game fish. Comes to the surface to eat, bringing larger items to eat at the shore. Uses its forepaws to manipulate, carry and tear apart food. Creates haul outs, well-worn trails leading from the water that often end up being littered with fish heads, scat and crayfish parts.

Likes to roll, which flattens areas of vegetation up to 6 feet (1.8 m) wide. Rolling areas have a musky odor from scent marking and usually contain some scat. Very vocal, giving a variety of sounds, such as a loud whistle, to communicate over long distances.

Male defends territory against other males. Female moves freely in and out of male territory. Digs den in a riverbank or lakeshore, often with an underwater entrance. May use an old beaver lodge. Has permanent and temporary dens. Permanent den, lined with leaves, grasses, mosses and hair, usually is where young are born.

Becomes sexually mature at 2-3 years. A male is generally solitary except during mating season and not around for the birth of the young. Returns in midsummer to help raise them.

237

Western Spotted Skunk
Spilogale gracilis

Family: Skunks (Mephitidae)

Size: L 9-12½" (22.5-32 cm); T 4½-7" (11-18 cm)

Weight: 1-1½ lb. (.5-.7 kg)

Description: White spot on head between eyes. Several stripes along the back and sides, some horizontal, some vertical, others broken into dashes and spots. Black tail with a white tip.

Origin/Age: native; 2-5 years

Compare: Much smaller than the Striped Skunk (pg. 243), which has 2 long white stripes on its back and a narrow white stripe between its eyes.

Habitat: woodlands, river bottoms, farmlands, woodland edges, shrublands, semideserts, fields, suburban and urban areas, canyons, mountainsides, elevations up to 8,000' (2,440 m)

Home: no regular burrow, mainly a rock crevice, hollow log or tree crevice, under a deck or porch

Food: omnivore; insects, spiders, small mammals, earthworms, grubs, bird eggs, amphibians, corn, fruit, berries, nuts, seeds, reptiles

Sounds: generally quiet, will stomp front feet and exhale in a loud "pfittt," also chatters its teeth

Breeding: Sep-Oct mating; 30-33 weeks gestation; implantation delayed until 20-30 days after mating

Young: 2-6 offspring once per year in April or May, born naked with black and white skin (matching the color of its future fur coat) and eyes closed, musky odor at 8-10 days, eyes open at about 30 days

Signs: pungent odor, more obvious when the skunk has sprayed, can be detected even if it has not sprayed; small, dark, segmented cylindrical scat, deposited on trails and at the entrance to den

Activity: mostly nocturnal; more active during summer than winter

Tracks: hind paw 1½" (4 cm) long with 5 toes and a well-defined heel pad, appearing flat-footed, forepaw 1" (2.5 cm) long and wide with 5 toes; 1 set of 4 tracks when bounding; fore and hind prints are very close together, 3-5" (7.5-13 cm) stride

Stan's Notes: It was reported in the early 1900s that this species was more common than the Striped Skunk (pg. 243) on the Western Slope in Colorado. Not common in any area now, with populations fluctuating widely. For reasons that are not known, populations of the Western Spotted Skunk and the very similar Eastern Spotted Skunk (not shown) have decreased dramatically all across the country. For a time, Western and Eastern Spotted Skunks were considered a single species, but now they are separated into two different species. The Western is the smaller of the two and has a larger white tip on its tail.

Fast, agile and adept at climbing trees. An expert mouser that, like a house cat, is good at controlling small mammal populations around ranches. Sometimes known as Civet Cat, but this name is misleading because it is neither a civet (mongoose, member of the Viverridae family), nor is it a cat. Considered by some people to have the softest fur of all animals.

Much more carnivorous than the Striped Skunk. Constantly on the move, looking for its next meal. Strictly nocturnal, extremely secretive and rarely seen.

When threatened it rushes forward, stomps its feet and stands on its forepaws with hind end elevated. Agile enough to spray from this position. Able to spray as far as 10 feet (3 m) with surprising accuracy. Odor is similar to that of the Striped Skunk.

Young are born in April and May. Young females are breeding at 4-5 months of age, which means they are mating by their first fall. Solitary except for breeding or when mothers have young.

Striped Skunk
Mephitis mephitis

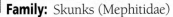

Family: Skunks (Mephitidae)

Size: L 20-24" (50-61 cm); T 7-14" (18-36 cm)

Weight: 6-12 lb. (2.7-5.4 kg)

Description: Black with 2 broad white stripes joined at head, separated along back or upper sides and blended into sides of tail. Thin white stripe down center of head between the ears and eyes. Large, bushy black tail with a white fringe and tip. Male larger than female.

Origin/Age: native; 2-5 years

Compare: Western Spotted Skunk (pg. 239) has a white spot on its face between the eyes. North American Porcupine (pg. 259) lacks white stripes.

Habitat: woodlands, river bottoms, farmlands, woodland edges, prairies, fields, suburban and urban areas, mountains, elevations up to 10,000' (3,050 m)

Home: burrow, often in hollow log or tree crevice, under a deck, porch, firewood or rock pile in summer

Food: omnivore; insects, spiders, small mammals, earthworms, grubs, bird eggs, amphibians, corn, fruit, berries, nuts, seeds, reptiles

Sounds: generally quiet, will stomp front feet and exhale in a loud "pfittt," also chatters its teeth

Breeding: Feb-Apr mating; 62-66 days gestation; implantation delayed until 18-20 days after mating

Young: 4-7 offspring once per year; born naked with black and white skin (matching the color of its future fur coat) and eyes closed, musky odor at 8-10 days, eyes open at about 24 days

babies in burrow   juvenile

Signs: pungent odor, more obvious when the skunk has sprayed, can be detected even when it has not sprayed; segmented cylindrical scat, often dark, deposited on trails and at entrance to the den

scat

Activity: mostly nocturnal; more active during summer than winter

Tracks: hind paw 2-3½" (5-9 cm) long with 5 toes and a well-defined heel pad, appearing flat-footed, forepaw 1-1¾" (2.5-4.5 cm) long and wide with 5 toes; alternating fore and hind prints are very close together when walking, 4-6" (10-15 cm) stride

Stan's Notes: Bred in the early 1900s for its fur, which explains the wide variety of colors in pet skunks today. The white stripes, which vary in length and width from one animal to another, can be used to identify individuals. Some have such wide stripes that they appear to be all white, although most are not albino.

The prominent black and white markings warn predators that it should not be approached. Will face a predator when threatened, arch its back and raise its tail while chattering its teeth. If this does not deter the predator, it will rush forward, stomp its feet, stand on forepaws with tail elevated and spray an oily, odorous yellow substance from glands at the base of its tail near the anus. Able to spray 5-6 times up to 15 feet (4.5 m) with surprising accuracy. This substance can cause temporary blindness and intense pain if it enters the eyes. Holding the animal by its tail off the ground will not prevent it from spraying.

This is a solitary, secretive skunk that wanders around in a slow, shuffling waddle in search of food. Does not hibernate, but will hole up in its burrow for several weeks to two months during cold, snowy weather. Has been known to burrow in groups of up to 15 individuals, often all females. This can be a problem when the burrow is under a house because of the cumulative smell.

spraying

Genus and species names mean "bad odor" and refer to the spray.

Ringtail
Bassariscus astutus

Family: Raccoons (Procyonidae)

Size: L 12-15½" (30-39 cm); T 12-16" (30-40 cm)

Weight: 2-2½ lb. (.9-1.1 kg)

Description: Cat-like in shape. Overall yellowish gray with long dark guard hairs, giving it a grizzled appearance. Small head with large pointed ears, like a fox. Very large dark eyes with a white ring around each eye. Large tail with 7-8 black and white or brown and white rings and a black tip.

Origin/Age: native; 6-10 years

Compare: Smaller and thinner than the Northern Raccoon (pg. 251), which has a distinctive black mask and shorter tail.

Habitat: canyonlands, semideserts, scrublands, elevations up to 9,000' (2,745 m)

Home: hollow tree, rock crevices, or underground den where trees are absent, den is lined with grasses and leaves

Food: omnivore; crayfish, fish, reptiles, amphibians, nuts, fruit, green leaves, suet, bird eggs, insects, small mammals such as mice, ground squirrels and baby birds

Sounds: snarls, growls and barks as alarm and threat calls

Breeding: Feb-Jun mating; 54-65 days gestation; female in heat (estrus) for only 3-6 days

Young: 1-5 offspring once per year, often in May or June; born with eyes closed, leaves den at 7-8 weeks

Signs: elongated cylindrical scat of various sizes and shapes, often placed in just one place, creating large common latrines to mark territories

Activity: nocturnal; active year-round except during cold snaps in winter

Tracks: hind paw 2¼-3" (5.5-7.5 cm) long with 5 long toes and no claw marks, forepaw 1½-2" (4-5 cm) long, slightly longer than wide with 5 distinct toes and no claw marks; tracks rarely seen because of the rocky habitat

Stan's Notes: A unique animal in Colorado that has a body like a cat, face and ears like a fox, a tail like a raccoon and climbs like a squirrel. An excellent mouser, once captured to control rodent populations in mines and referred to as Miner's Cat. Also known as Ringtail Cat, Civet Cat or Rock Cat. Another common name, Cacomistle, coming from the Mexican Nahuatl Indians, translates to "half mountain lion."

This animal is an excellent climber, with sharp claws that facilitate climbing trees and large rocks. The hind feet rotate 180 degrees, allowing it to climb down trees and rocks like a squirrel, face first. Can also jump across great distances, similar to squirrels.

A nocturnal critter and an expert hunter, bringing down a wide variety of mice, ground squirrels, woodrats and other small mammals, along with lizards and large insects. Pounces on prey and kills it, biting the base of the neck, and eats meals headfirst.

Not much is known about the distribution. Recent studies find it might be more common and widespread than was previously noted. Unknown social structure, but some individuals hunt and travel together where ranges overlap.

Males mark their territories with urine. Anal glands in both sexes give off a foul odor when the animal is threatened or alarmed.

Northern Raccoon

Procyon lotor

Family: Raccoons (Procyonidae)

Size: L 24-25" (61-64 cm); T 7-16" (18-40 cm)

Weight: 12-35 lb. (5.4-15.8 kg)

Description: Overall gray to brown, sometimes nearly black to silver. Distinctive black band across face (mask), eyes and down to the chin. White snout. Bushy, black-tipped brown tail with 4-6 evenly spaced dark bands or rings.

Origin/Age: native; 6-10 years

Compare: Very distinctive animal. The black mask and dark rings on the tail make it hard to confuse with any other species.

Habitat: almost all habitats, rural and urban, but mostly wetlands, elevations up to 10,000' (3,050 m)

Home: hollow tree, or underground den where trees are absent

Food: omnivore; crayfish, fish, reptiles, amphibians, nuts, fruit, green leaves, suet, birdseed (especially black-oil sunflower seeds and thistle), small mammals, baby birds, bird eggs, insects

Sounds: very loud snarls, growls, hisses and screams are common (and may be frightening) during the mating season, soft purring sounds and quiet chuckles between mothers and babies

Breeding: Feb-Jun mating; 54-65 days gestation; female in heat (estrus) for only 3-6 days

Young: 3-6 offspring per year, usually in May; born with eyes closed, leaves den at 7-8 weeks

Signs: pile of half-digested berries deposited on a log, rock, under a bird feeder or on top of a garbage can; scat is usually cylindrical, 2" (5 cm) long and ¾" (2 cm) wide, but can be highly variable due to diet

scat

Activity: nocturnal; active year-round except during cold snaps in winter

Tracks: hind paw 3½-4½" (9-11 cm) long with 5 long toes and claw marks, forepaw 2½-3" (6-7.5 cm) long, slightly longer than wide with 5 distinct toes and claw marks; forepaws land (register) next to hind prints, 8-20" (20-50 cm) stride

Stan's Notes: Raccoons are native only to the Americas from Central America to the United States and lower Canada. The Northern Raccoon is found statewide in Colorado. Common name comes from the Algonquian Indian word *arougbcoune*, meaning "he scratches with his hands." Known for the ability to open such objects as doors, coolers and latches. Uses its nimble fingers to feel around the edges of ponds, rivers and lakes for crayfish and frogs. Known to occasionally wash its food before eating, hence the species name *lotor*, meaning "washer." However, it is not washing its food, but kneading and tearing it apart. The water helps it feel the parts that are edible and those that are not. A strong swimmer.

juveniles

Able to climb any tree very quickly and can come down headfirst or tail end first. Its nails can grip bark no matter which way it climbs because it can rotate its hind feet nearly 180 degrees so that the hind toes always point up the tree.

Active at night, sleeping in hollow trees or other dens during the day. Often mistakenly associated with forests, but also lives in prairies, using underground dens.

Usually a solitary animal as an adult. Does not hibernate but will sleep or simply hole up in a comfortable den from January to February. Will occasionally den in small groups of the same sex, usually males, or females without young.

Emerging from winter sleep, males wander many miles in search of a mate. Females use the same den for several months while raising their young, but move out afterward and find a new place to sleep each night. Males are not involved in raising young. Young remain with the adult female for nearly a year.

Nine-banded Armadillo

Dasypus novemcinctus

Family: Armadillos, Sloths and Anteaters (Dasypodidae)

Size: L 15-21" (38-53 cm); T 9-14" (22.5-36 cm)

Weight: 8-17 lb. (3.6-7.7 kg)

Description: Unique-looking round body covered in 9 heavy bony plates (armor). Each scale looks like it is comprised of small scales. Tan to brown, usually covered in mud, but can be shiny. Long, narrow pointed snout. Tiny eyes and tall oval ears. Short legs. Long nails. Long narrow tail, lacking hair.

Origin/Age: native; 4-7 years

Compare: Hard to confuse with any other animal. Opossum (pg. 263) has a furred body. Look for segmented body armor and a hairless tail to help identify.

Habitat: grasslands, open woodlands, scrublands, wetlands

Home: burrow, several entrances with little excavated dirt, sometimes at the base of a rock, usually in a small hill or riverbank, up to 15' (4.5 m) long and 3' (1 m) deep, 1 chamber lined with vegetation

Food: omnivore; mainly insects; also eats the carrion of rabbits, squirrels, snakes, lizards and frogs

Sounds: sniffing noises, several grunts and groans

Breeding: Jul-Aug mating; 115-120 days gestation; implantation delayed until late October or November

Young: up to 6 offspring once per year; born with eyes open and shell intact (although not hardened), young often genetically identical, with 4 (quadruplets) the most common number produced from a single fertilized egg, weaned at about 3 months

tail

Signs: burrow entrance that is 6-8" (15-20 cm) wide; round gray pellets, ¾" (2 cm) wide, resembling clay marbles due to the amount of soil consumed while digging up insects

Activity: diurnal, nocturnal; can be seen at many times of the day and night, does not come out on cold, rainy days

Tracks: hind paw 2" (5 cm) long with 5 toes, forepaw 1½-1¾" (4-4.5 cm) long, with 4 toes; 1 set of 4 tracks; hind paws fall slightly behind fore prints; tracks often in a straight line, 4-6" (10-15 cm) stride with a partial tail drag mark, seen in dry dirt and mud along streams and wetlands

Stan's Notes: Member of an order of animals with unique backbone joints that allow them to bend more than animals that have backbones without special joints. Animals in this group are seen only in the New World, in South, Central and North America. While there are several armadillo species, only the Nine-banded is found in North America.

Expanding its range in the United States, having moved up from Mexico, and has been introduced into Arkansas, Florida and other areas of the country. Needs to drink water every day and is limited in Colorado by the lack of freestanding water. It is not very common here, with only a few specimens recorded.

Gets the common name "Nine" from the number of armored, jointed (articulated) plates on its body. Able to curl up tightly, with the plate on top of its head protecting the joint where the front and back of the armored shell meet. When threatened, the first defense of an armadillo is to run off or hide in its burrow, where it lodges itself, using its armor as protection. Armored up inside a burrow makes it nearly impossible to pull the animal out. If the burrow is not near, it will curl up to shield itself.

Eyesight is not that great, so sometimes it stands upright to sniff the air for danger, supporting itself with its tail. Spends most of its time out of the burrow with its nose to the ground, sniffing for insects or other food. An excellent excavator, digging under fallen logs or tearing apart logs, using its short, thick, powerful legs and long toe nails to burrow and search out food.

Young can walk within hours of birth. Appearing like miniature piglets, they follow their mother around in a line, single file.

North American Porcupine

Erethizon dorsatum

Family: Porcupine (Erethizontidae)

Size: L 20-26" (50-66 cm); T 6-12" (15-30 cm)

Weight: 7-30 lb. (3.2-13.5 kg)

Description: A short, stocky body with short legs, an arching back and quills on rump and tail. Dark brown to nearly black. Longest guard hairs are often white-tipped. Ears are small, round and barely visible. Tiny dark eyes. Small feet with long claws.

Origin/Age: native; 5-10 years

Compare: Similar size as Striped Skunk (pg. 243), but lacks white stripes. Look for the obvious body shape (arching back) and large white-tipped quills to identify. Can be seen on the ground or in trees.

Habitat: coniferous and deciduous forests, prairies, yards, up to the tree line at 10,000' (3,050 m)

Home: den in a large hollow tree or a fallen hollow log, underground burrow

Food: herbivore; soft bark, inner bark of conifers, green plants, tree leaves, leaf buds

Sounds: much vocalization with loud, shrill screeching during mating, mothers make soft grunts and groans to communicate with their babies

Breeding: Oct-Nov mating; 7 months gestation; female is receptive to mating (estrus) for only 8-12 hours; has a very long gestation period for a rodent

Young: 1 offspring once per year in May or June; born fully quilled with teeth erupted and eyes open, feeds itself within 1 week, weaned by 1 month, stays with mother until the first autumn

juvenile

Signs: large pieces of bark gnawed from conifer trunks, tooth marks on exposed wood, cleanly chewed twigs and branches laying nearby, chew marks on buildings, canoe paddles and ax handles; pile of pellets, often irregular in size and shape due to diet, may have soft segmented scat in summer, hard individual pellets in winter

scat

Activity: mostly nocturnal, crepuscular; active year-round

Tracks: hind paw 3-3½" (7.5-9 cm) long, wide oval with claw marks and dotted (stippled) impression from rough, pebbled pads, forepaw 2-2½" (5-6 cm) long, oval with claw marks; 1 set of 2 tracks; fore and hind prints alternate left and right with toes pointing inward, hind paws fall near or onto fore prints, tail drag mark between each set of prints in mud or deep snow

Stan's Notes: A slow, solitary animal that is usually seen sleeping at the top of a tree or slowly crossing a road. Makes up for its slow speed by protecting itself with long, barb-tipped guard hairs that are solid at the tip and base and hollow in between. It has over 30,000 sharp quills, which actually are modified hairs loosely attached to a sheet of muscles just beneath the skin. Unable to throw the quills, but will swing and hit with its tail, driving the tail quills deep into even the toughest flesh. Some report that quill barbs are heat sensitive and open when entering flesh, making them very hard to extract. Quills provide such an excellent defense, only few predators are capable of killing a porcupine.

Uses a den in a large tree for sleeping during the day or for holing up for several days or weeks during cold snaps in winter. Feeds on inner bark of coniferous trees in winter, but moves to the ground to eat green vegetation in spring and summer.

Males find females during the mating season by sniffing the base of trees and rocks where a female might have passed. Males can become very aggressive toward other males, often fighting during the breeding season.

Elaborate mating with much vocalization and several males often attending one female. When the female is ready to mate, she will raise her tail to permit typical mounting.

Babies have an atypical birth, emerging headfirst with eyes open, teeth erupted and covered with quills. Quills are soft and dry and become stiff within a couple hours.

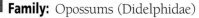

Virginia Opossum
Didelphis virginiana

Family: Opossums (Didelphidae)

Size: L 25-30" (64-76 cm); T 10-20" (25-50 cm)

Weight: 4-14 lb. (1.8-6.3 kg)

Description: Gray-to-brown body, sometimes nearly black. A white head, throat and belly. Long narrow snout and wide mouth. Oval, naked black ears. Long, scaly, semiprehensile, naked pinkish tail. Short legs. Feet have 5 toes. First toe on hind feet is thumb-like and lacks a nail. Pink nose and toes.

Origin/Age: native; 3-5 years

Compare: Muskrat (pg. 79) is much smaller, all brown and rarely far from water. Norway Rat (pg. 67) also has a long naked tail, but Virginia Opossum is larger and nearly white with large dark ears and a pink nose. Norway Rat is rarely seen in trees.

Habitat: deciduous forests, farmlands, wetlands, prairies, yards, cities, elevations below 6,000' (1,830 m)

Home: leaf nest in an underground den or hollow log

Food: omnivore; insects, sunflower and Nyjer thistle seeds, nuts, berries, fruit, leaves, bird eggs, fish, reptiles, amphibians, small mammals, road kill, earthworms

Sounds: low growls, hisses and shows teeth if threatened, soft clicks between mothers and young

Breeding: Jan-Feb mating; 8-14 days gestation

Young: 2-13 (usually 5-6) offspring once per year; newborns the size of a navy bean crawl to mother's external fur-lined pouch, where they attach to a nipple for as long as 2 months

Signs: overturned garbage cans; scat on ground under sunflower seed and Nyjer thistle feeders

scat

Activity: nocturnal; can be seen during the day in the coldest part of winter

Tracks: hind paw 2" (5 cm) long with 5 toes, large thumb-like first toe points inward and lacks a nail, forepaw 1½" (4 cm) long with 5 toes spread out; fore and hind prints are parallel, 7" (18 cm) stride, often has a tail drag mark

Stan's Notes: The Virginia Opossum is the only marsupial found north of Mexico. Having expanded its range in Colorado over the past 50 years, it is now seen along most major rivers and in most large cities in lower elevations.

A unique-looking animal, the size of a house cat. It has 50 teeth, more than any other mammal in Colorado. The tip of its naked pink tail and ears often get frostbite during winter, turn black and fall off.

Usually solitary, moving around on the ground from place to place. Also climbs trees well, using its tail to aid in climbing, holding onto branches (semiprehensile). An adult opossum cannot hang by the tail like a monkey, but the young seem able to, perhaps due to their lighter weight.

Frequently feeds on dead animals along roads and is often hit by cars. Not a fast mover, will hiss if threatened and show its short, pointy teeth. When that doesn't work, often rolls over and feigns death with eyes closed, mouth open and tongue hanging out, "playing 'possum." Does not hibernate, but sleeps in dens for weeks during the coldest part of winter.

Males give loud, aggressive displays during the breeding season and will scent-mark by licking themselves and rubbing their heads against tree trunks or other stationary objects. Young ride on their mother's back after weaning.

Opossums can defend themselves against large predators and survive substantial injuries. One study showed nearly half of all examined dead opossums had healed broken bones, some with multiple fractures. Many opossums are immune to venomous snake bites and have a resistance to rabies and plague.

Kit Fox
Vulpes macrotis

Family: Wolves, Foxes and Coyote (Canidae)

Size: L 15-21" (38-53 cm); T 9-12" (22.5-30 cm); H 10-12" (25-30 cm)

Weight: 3-7 lb. (1.4-3.2 kg)

Description: Yellowish tan fox with a dark line down the back and onto tail. White chin and upper neck. White to tan on the belly. Extremely large, pointed ears. Long thin legs, same color as the body.

Origin/Age: native, 5-10 years

Compare: The Swift Fox (pg. 271) is very similar, but has a shorter tail, shorter muzzle and slightly smaller ears. Best to use range to help distinguish the Kit from the Swift. The Gray Fox (pg. 275) is larger, darker and has shorter ears. Red Fox (pg. 279) is larger and has red fur with a white-tipped tail.

Habitat: semideserts, canyons, prairies, open fields, elevations below 6,000' (1,830 m)

Home: underground den, sometimes a hollow log or in a hillside or stream bank, with 3-4 entrances, often with a dirt mound up to 3' (1 m) high with scat and scraps of food in front of main entrance; may have several den sites in its territory

Food: omnivore; small mammals such as rabbits, hares, mice, moles, woodrats and voles; also eats fish, berries, apples, nuts, insects and carrion

Sounds: hoarse high-pitched barks, yelps to steady high-pitched screams, mournful cries

Breeding: winter (Jan-Mar) mating; 51-53 days gestation

Young: 1-8 kits once per year in April or May

267

Signs: cylindrical scat with a tapered end, frequently contains hair and bones, often found on a trail, prominent rock or stump or at the den entrance

Activity: mainly nocturnal, crepuscular; can be seen during the day around the den site, sunning itself

Tracks: forepaw 1½" (4 cm) long, oval, with hind paw slightly smaller; 4 toes on each foot, straight line of single tracks; hind paws fall near or directly onto fore prints (direct register) when walking, often obliterating the forepaw tracks, 8-12" (20-30 cm) stride when walking

Stan's Notes: The Kit Fox, along with the Swift Fox (pg. 271), is considered the smallest of our wild dogs, having the approximate size of a house cat. Once considered the same species as the Swift Fox, the Kit in Colorado is restricted to locations in the far western edge of the state. One small population has been located near Delta and Montrose Counties. Listed as an endangered species in Colorado, but widespread in the southwestern United States, extending from Nevada to California, Arizona, New Mexico and farther south into Mexico.

Highly specialized, surviving in semidesert environments. Does not require a constant supply of fresh water, obtaining all the moisture it needs from its prey and through water conservation, achieved by the production of a specialized urine that is low in water content.

In Colorado, the Kit Fox seems to depend greatly on rabbits and hares for food. Fleet of foot, it runs very fast for short distances, allowing it to capture other swift prey such as rabbits.

Digs its own den (semifossorial) down as far as 8 feet (2.4 m), fashioning it with many entrances. Doesn't hibernate. Mates pair up in late winter when females clean out dens and get ready to breed. Young first emerge at the den entrance at 5-6 weeks of age. Some report that helper females take part in raising the young of older females.

Some pairs have long-term pair bonds; others don't. Males will bring food to the female while she is nursing young. At weaning, both adults hunt for food and bring it back to the den. Parents carry prey whole to the den and don't regurgitate food.

Swift Fox
Vulpes velox

Family: Wolves, Foxes and Coyote (Canidae)

Size: L 15-21" (38-53 cm); T 9-12" (22.5-30 cm); H 10-12" (25-30 cm)

Weight: 3-7 lb. (1.4-3.2 kg)

Description: Yellowish tan fox with a grayish back and sides. White chin and upper neck. White to tan on the belly. Large pointed ears. Small dark marks in front of each eye. Long, bushy black-tipped tail.

Origin/Age: native, 5-10 years

Compare: Kit Fox (pg. 267) has a longer tail, larger muzzle and taller ears; Kit is less common and seen only in far western Colorado unlike the Swift, which is found in the eastern half of the state. The Gray Fox (pg. 275) is larger, darker and has shorter ears. The Red Fox (pg. 279) is larger and has red fur with a white-tipped tail.

Habitat: semideserts, grasslands, prairies, open fields, elevations below 6,000' (1,830 m)

Home: underground den, in a hillside, cliff or bank of a stream, 3-4 entrances, often a dirt mound up to 3' (1 m) high at the main entrance with scat and food scraps; may have several dens in its territory

Food: carnivorous; small animals such as rabbits, hares, mice, moles, woodrats and voles; also eats carrion

Sounds: hoarse high-pitched barks, yelps, high-pitched screams, mournful cries

Breeding: winter (Jan-Feb) mating; 50-53 days gestation

Young: 1-8 kits once per year in March, April or early May; born helpless with eyes closed

271

Signs: cylindrical scat with a tapered end, frequently contains hair and bones, often found on a trail, prominent rock or stump or at the den entrance

Activity: mainly nocturnal, crepuscular; can be seen during the day around the den site, sunning itself

Tracks: forepaw 1½" (4 cm) long, oval, with hind paw slightly smaller; 4 toes on each foot, straight line of single tracks; hind paws fall near or directly onto fore prints (direct register) when walking, often obliterating the forepaw tracks, 8-12" (20-30 cm) stride when walking

Stan's Notes: A species of special concern in Colorado. The Swift Fox was once considered to be the same species as the Kit Fox (pg. 267), but now is a separate species. The Swift is by far more common in the state than the Kit and can be seen in the eastern half of Colorado, where there is flat terrain or gentle rolling hills.

Usually seen in pairs and occasionally with more adults together. It is unclear whether or not Swift Foxes mate for life. An excellent digger (semifossorial), it creates several dens and moves its young from den to den when they are old enough to follow their parents.

Often associated with prairie dog towns and jackrabbits in grasslands. Unlike the Red Fox (pg. 279) or Gray Fox (pg. 275), the Swift is largely carnivorous, feeding mainly on cottontail rabbits and jackrabbits, which are nearly the same size as itself, if not slightly taller. When a Swift catches more than it can eat, it will cache the food in shallow depressions, covering the leftovers with a scant amount of dirt. Does not hibernate.

The young are born helpless with eyes closed. They grow quickly, opening their eyes at 10-14 days and appearing aboveground at 4-5 weeks of age. They learn to hunt from their parents and are dispersed from their home den at the end of their first summer. Young females are capable of breeding in their first year.

Gray Fox
Urocyon cinereoargenteus

Family: Wolves, Foxes and Coyote (Canidae)

Size: L 22-24" (56-61 cm); T 10-17" (25-43 cm); H 14-15" (36-38 cm)

Weight: 7-13 lb. (3.2-5.9 kg)

Description: Grizzled gray fox with a rust red nape, shoulders and rust red across the chest. Large pointed ears, trimmed in white. White chin, neck and belly. Large bushy tail with a black tip and ridge of stiff dark hairs along the top.

Origin/Age: native; 5-10 years

Compare: Less common than the Red Fox (pg. 279), which has a white-tipped tail. Coyote (pg. 283) shares the grayish appearance and black-tipped tail, but is larger than the Gray Fox and has longer legs.

Habitat: deciduous forests, rocky outcrops, river valleys, brush areas, elevations up to 7,500' (2,285 m)

Home: den, mostly in a natural cavity such as a log or a crevice in rock, will enlarge a prairie dog burrow, unlike a Red Fox den, the den of a Gray Fox lacks a mound of dirt in front of the entrance

Food: omnivore; small mammals such as mice, moles, voles, rabbits and hares; also eats berries, apples, nuts, fish, insects and carrion

Sounds: hoarse high-pitched barks, yelps to steady high-pitched screams, mournful cries; much less vocal than the Red Fox

Breeding: winter (Jan-Mar) mating; 51-53 days gestation

Young: 1-7 kits once per year in April or May; born helpless with black fur and eyes closed

275

scat

Signs: urine and piles of feces, mostly on conspicuous landmarks such as a prominent rock, stump or trail; cylindrical scat with a tapered end, can be very dark if berries were eaten, often contains hair and bones

Activity: mostly nocturnal, crepuscular; can be seen during the day in winter, especially when overcast

Tracks: forepaw 1½" (4 cm) long, oval, hind paw slightly smaller; straight line of single tracks; hind paws fall near or directly onto fore prints (direct register) when walking, often obliterating the forepaw tracks, 10-14" (25-36 cm) stride when walking

Stan's Notes: The scientific name of the Gray Fox provides a very good description of the animal. The genus name *Urocyon* is Greek for "tailed dog." Species name *cinereoargenteus* is Latin and means "silver" or "gray and black."

Also called Treefox because it often climbs trees. Climbs to escape larger predators more than it does to find food. Sometimes it will rest in a tree. Shinnies up, pivoting its front legs at the shoulder joints to grab the trunk and pushes with hind feet. Able to rotate its front legs more than other canids. Once up the trunk, it jumps from branch to branch and has been seen up to 20 feet (6.1 m) high. Descends by backing down or running headfirst down a sloping branch.

Thought to mate for life. Male often travels 50 miles (81 km) to establish territory. A pair will defend a territory of 2-3 square miles (5-8 sq. km).

The kits are weaned at about six weeks. Male doesn't enter the den, but helps feed the family by bringing in food. Young disperse at the end of summer just before the parents start mating again.

Red Fox
Vulpes vulpes

Family: Wolves, Foxes and Coyote (Canidae)

Size: L 22-24" (56-61 cm); T 13-17" (33-43 cm); H 15-16" (38-40 cm)

Weight: 7-15 lb. (3.2-6.8 kg)

Description: Usually rusty red with dark highlights, but can vary from light yellow to black. Large pointed ears trimmed in black with white inside. White jowls, chest and belly. Legs nearly black. Large bushy tail with a white tip. Fluffy coat in winter and spring. Molts by July, appearing smaller and thinner.

Origin/Age: native, 5-10 years

Compare: Gray Fox (pg. 275) is not as red and has a black-tipped tail. Smaller than the Coyote (pg. 283), usually more red and has a white-tipped tail. All other wild canids lack a tail with a white tip.

Habitat: forests, prairies, rangelands, cities, suburbs, foothills, mountains, all elevations

Home: den, sometimes a hollow log, may dig a den under a log or a rock in a bank of a stream or in a hillside created when land was cut to build a road, often has a mound of dirt up to 3' (1 m) high in front of the main entrance with scat deposits

Food: omnivore; small mammals such as mice, moles, voles, rabbits and hares; also eats berries, apples, nuts, fish, insects and carrion

Sounds: hoarse high-pitched barks, yelps to steady high-pitched screams, mournful cries

Breeding: winter (Jan-Mar) mating; 51-53 days gestation

Young: 1-10 kits once per year in April or May

summer coat

winter coat

silver morph dark morph

scat

Signs: cylindrical scat with a tapered end, can be very dark if berries were eaten, frequently contains hair and bones, often found on a trail, prominent rock or stump or at den entrance

Activity: mainly nocturnal, crepuscular; rests during the middle of the night

Tracks: forepaw 2" (5 cm) long, oval, with hind paw slightly smaller; straight line of single tracks; hind paws fall near or directly onto fore prints (direct register) when walking, often obliterating the forepaw tracks, 10-14" (25-36 cm) stride when walking

Stan's Notes: The most widely distributed of wild canids in the world, ranging across North America, Asia, Europe and northern Africa. European Red Foxes were introduced into North America in the 1790s, resulting in some confusion regarding the original distribution and lineage.

Usually alone. Very intelligent and learns from past experiences. Often catlike in behavior, pouncing on prey. Sleeps at the base of a tree or rock, even in winter, curling itself up into a ball.

den entrance

Hunts for mice, moles and other small prey by stalking, looking and listening. Hearing differs from the other mammals. Hears low-frequency sounds, enabling it to detect small mammals digging and gnawing underground. Chases larger prey such as rabbits and squirrels. Hunts even if full, caching extra food underground or burying it in snow. Finds cached food using its memory and sense of smell.

Mated pairs will actively defend their territory from other foxes; however, they are often killed by coyotes or wolves. Uses a den only several weeks for birthing and raising young. Parents bring food to kits in the den. At first, parents regurgitate the food. Later, they will bring fresh meat and live prey to the den, allowing the kits to practice killing. Young are dispersed at the end of their first summer, with the males (dog foxes) traveling 100-150 miles (161-242 km), much farther than females (vixens), to establish their own territories.

kits

Coyote
Canis latrans

Family: Wolves, Foxes and Coyote (Canidae)

Size: L 3-3½' (1-1.1 m); T 12-15" (30-38 cm); H 2' (61 cm)

Weight: 20-40 lb. (9-18 kg)

Description: Tan fur with black and orange highlights. Large, pointed reddish orange ears with white interior. Long narrow snout with a white upper lip. Long legs and bushy black-tipped tail.

Origin/Age: native; 5-10 years

Compare: Smaller than Gray Wolf (pg. 287) with larger ears and narrower pointed snout. Red Fox (pg. 279) has black legs and a white-tipped tail.

Habitat: urban, suburban and rural areas, forests, fields, farms, mountains, elevations up to 12,000' (3,660 m)

Home: den, usually in a riverbank, hillside, under a rock or tree root, entrance 1-2' (30-61 cm) high, can be up to 30' (9.1 m) deep and ends in small chamber where female gives birth; female may dig own den or enlarge a fox or badger den

Food: omnivore; small mammals, reptiles, amphibians, birds, bird eggs, insects, fruit, carrion

Sounds: barks like a dog, calls to others result in a chorus of high-pitched howling and yipping; sounds different from the lower, deeper call of the Gray Wolf, which rarely yips

Breeding: midwinter to late winter mating; 63 days average gestation

Young: 4-6 pups once per year in April or May; born with eyes closed

summer coat

winter coat

scat

Signs: cylindrical scat (shape is similar to that of domestic dog excrement), often containing fur and bones, along well-worn game trails, on prominent rocks and at trail intersections

Activity: nocturnal, crepuscular, diurnal; can be seen for several hours after sunrise and before sunset

Tracks: forepaw 2¼" (5.5 cm) long, round to slightly oval, hind paw slightly smaller; straight line of single tracks; hind paws fall near or directly onto fore prints (direct register) when walking, often obliterating the forepaw tracks, 12-15" (30-38 cm) stride when walking, 24-30" (61-76 cm) stride when running

Stan's Notes: Sometimes called Brush Wolf or Prairie Wolf, even though this animal is obviously not a wolf. The genus name *Canis* is Latin for "dog." The species name *latrans* is also Latin and means "barking." It is believed that the common name "Coyote" comes from the Aztec word *coyotl*, which means "barking dog."

Frequently seen as a gluttonous outlaw, this animal is only guilty of being able to survive a rapidly changing environment and outright slaughter by humans. Intelligent and playful, much like the domestic dog. Hunts alone or in small groups. Uses its large ears to hear small mammals beneath snow or vegetation. Stands over a spot, cocks its head back and forth to pinpoint prey and then pounces. Will also chase larger prey such as rabbits.

Most coyotes run with their tails down unlike dogs and wolves, which run with their tails level to upright. A fast runner, it can travel 25-30 mph (40-48 km/h). May reach 40 mph (64 km/h) for short distances. Some coyotes tracked with radio collars are known to travel more than 400 miles (644 km) over several days.

Often courts for 2-3 months before mating. A monogamous animal, with mated pairs staying together for many years or for life.

Pups emerge from the den at 2-3 weeks and are weaned at 5-7 weeks. Mother will move her pups from the den when she feels threatened. Mother often gets help raising young from other group members and her mate. Pups do not return to the den once they are able to survive on their own. Mother abandons the den once the pups leave and will often return year after year in spring to use the same den.

RARE

Gray Wolf
Canis lupus

Family: Wolves, Foxes and Coyote (Canidae)

Size: L 4-5' (1.2-1.5 m); T 14-20" (36-50 cm); H 26-38" (66-96 cm)

Weight: 55-130 lb. (25-59 kg)

Description: Usually gray with dark highlights, but can vary from all white to entirely black. A large bushy tail, almost always black-tipped. Short pointed ears. Long legs. Male is slightly larger than female.

Origin/Age: native; 5-15 years

Compare: Larger than Coyote (pg. 283) and has longer legs and shorter ears. Often holds its tail straight out when traveling compared with the Coyote, which holds its tail at a downward angle.

Habitat: deciduous and coniferous forests, prairies

Home: shelter or den only for raising young, den can be 5-15' (1.5-4.5 m) deep, frequently more than 1 entrance, fan of dirt at entrance, often scattered bones and fur laying about; used for many years

Food: omnivore; small to large mammals such as mice, rabbits, hares, deer, moose and bears; also eats berries, grass, insects and fish

Sounds: yelps, barks and howls, howling may rise and fall in pitch or remain the same, rarely has a series of yips or yelps at the end, like the Coyote

Breeding: Jan-Feb mating; 63-65 days gestation

Young: 1-10 pups once per year; born helpless with eyes closed, wide range of color variations, some look like the parents, others are completely different, remains the same color its entire life

white morph

black morph

gray morph

pups

Signs: scrapes in the dirt, urine on posts, rocks and stumps; scat looks like the excrement of a domestic dog, but it is larger and contains hairs and bone fragments

scat

Activity: nocturnal, more diurnal in winter; hunts at night in summer

Tracks: forepaw 5½-6½" (14-16 cm) long, hind paw slightly smaller, both round with clear claw marks; straight line of single tracks; hind paws fall near or directly onto fore prints (direct register) when walking, often obliterating the forepaw tracks, 15-30" (38-76 cm) stride; rarely walks along roads like a domestic dog

Stan's Notes: Largest wild dog species. Formerly ranged in the northern states, but was exterminated from most places. Now found in many areas including Wyoming, Minnesota, Wisconsin and Michigan. No known population exists in Colorado. Has been under consideration for reintroduction. Individuals may wander into the state. Shies away from humans.

One of the most mobile animals, traveling great distances to find food each day. Eats 3-5 pounds (1.4-2.3 kg) of meat per day, but can go weeks without food. May cache large prey items. Not a good long distance runner, but able to achieve speeds of 30 mph (48 km/h) for short distances. A good swimmer, following prey into the water or swimming to islands in lakes and rivers. Communicates by howling, body posturing and scent marking.

This is a social animal, living in packs of 2-15 individuals that consist primarily of family members. The pack has a well-defined hierarchy with a sole male leader called alpha and his female mate, also alpha.

Territory of a pack frequently covers 100-300 square miles (260-780 sq. km). Often uses the same well-worn trails in some areas. Territories of other packs may overlap, but conflicts rarely occur when food is plentiful.

Packs work together to hunt, chasing down prey or ambushing. Dominant members feed first. Some adults bring food back in their stomachs to pups, since mothers will not leave them for the first month. Pups will mob and lick the faces of feeder adults, encouraging regurgitation of food. When pups are older, some pack members baby-sit while the alpha pair goes hunting with the rest of the pack. Young join the pack to hunt in the fall of their first year, and leave the pack at 2-3 years to form their own or join another. After the pups leave, the pack will rendezvous before and after hunting, usually at a grassy area with a good view of the surroundings.

Bobcat
Lynx rufus

Family: Cats (Felidae)

Size: L 2¼-3½' (69-107 cm); T 3-7" (7.5-18 cm); H 2' (61 cm)

Weight: 14-30 lb. (6.3-13.5 kg)

Description: Tawny brown during summer. Light gray during winter with dark streaks and spots. Long stiff fur projects down from jowls and tapers to a point (ruffs). Triangular ears, tipped with short black hairs (tufts). Prominent white spot on the back of ears. Dark horizontal barring on the upper legs. Short stubby tail with a black tip on the top and sides and a white underside. Male slightly larger than female.

Origin/Age: native; 10-15 years

Compare: Much smaller than the Mountain Lion (pg. 299), which has a long rope-like tail. The Canada Lynx (pg. 295) is larger, with long ear tufts and a black-tipped tail. Look for long ear tufts and a white underside on the tail to help identify the Bobcat.

Habitat: mixed forests, fields, farmlands, elevations up to 12,000' (3,660 m)

Home: den, often in a hollow log, rock crevice or under a pile of tree branches filled with leaves

Food: carnivore; medium to small mammals such as rabbits and mice; also eats birds and carrion

Sounds: raspy meows and yelps, purrs when content

Breeding: Feb-Mar mating; 60-70 days gestation

Young: 1-7 (usually 3) kittens once per year in April or May

Signs: scratching posts with claw marks 3-4' (1-1.2 m) aboveground, caches of larger kills covered with a light layer of leaves and twigs, scent posts marked with urine (often seen only in winter when urine sprays onto snow); long cylindrical scat, contains hair and bones, often buried, sometimes visible under a thin layer of dirt and debris

scat

Activity: nocturnal, diurnal; often rests on hot days in a sheltered spot such as under a fallen log or in a rock crevice

Tracks: forepaw and hind paw 2" (5 cm), round, multi-lobed heel pad, 4 toes on all feet, lacking claw marks; straight line of tracks; hind paws fall near or on fore prints (direct register) when walking, often obliterating forepaw tracks, 9-13" (22.5-33 cm) stride

Stan's Notes: The most common wildcat species in Colorado. Much more common than the Canada Lynx (pg. 295), thriving in nearly all habitat types. The common name refers to the short, stubby or "bobbed" tail. Frequently walks with tail curled upward, which exposes the white underside, making this animal easy to identify. Makes sounds similar to a house cat.

Often uses the same trails in its territory to patrol for rabbits, which is its favorite food, and other prey. Does not climb trees as much as the Canada Lynx, but swims well. Hunts by stalking or laying in wait to attack (ambushing). Ambushes prey by rushing forward, chases and captures it, then kills it with a bite to the neck. Has been known to go without eating for several weeks during periods of famine.

Male has a larger territory than female. Usually solitary except for mating and when mothers are with young. Male will seek out a female in heat. Several males may follow a female until she is ready for mating.

Female does not breed until her second year. She has a primary (natal) den in which kittens are born and live for a short time after birth. Female also has secondary dens in her territory, where she may move her young if the natal den is disturbed. Dens are used only by the females and young. Mother raises young on her own.

kittens

Kittens are born well furred and with spots. Their eyes are closed at birth and open at about 10 days. They are weaned at approximately 8 weeks, when they start to hunt with their mother. Young stay with their mother until about 7 months, when she disperses them to mate.

Canada Lynx
Lynx canadensis

Family: Cats (Felidae)

Size: L 2½-4' (76-122 cm); T 2-5" (5-13 cm); H 2-2¼' (61-69 cm)

Weight: 20-40 lb. (9-18 kg)

Description: Light gray to brown overall. Small ears, 2" (5 cm) long, with black hairs that form a tuft. Long stiff fur projects downward from the jowls and tapers to a point (ruffs). Long legs. Large round feet. A black-tipped tail, as though dipped in ink. Male slightly larger than female.

Origin/Age: native; 10-15 years

Compare: Smaller than Mountain Lion (pg. 299), which has a long rope-like tail. Larger than the Bobcat (pg. 291), which has short ear tufts and a white underside on the tail. Look for long ear tufts and a black-tipped tail to identify the Canada Lynx.

Habitat: coniferous forests, rocky outcrops, elevations up to 13,000' (3,960 m)

Home: den, usually in a hollow log, rock crevice or on leaves under branches; used by female and young

Food: carnivore; medium to small mammals such as rabbits, hares, voles and mice; will also eat birds such as Ruffed Grouse and feed on carrion

Sounds: raspy meows and yelps, purrs when content, similar to a house cat

Breeding: Mar-Apr mating; 60-70 days gestation

Young: 1-5 (usually 3) kittens once per year or every 2 years; born blind and covered with spots and streaks, becomes uniformly brown at 1 year

kitten

scat

Signs: scratching posts with claw marks 3-4' (1-1.2 m) aboveground, caches of larger kills covered with a light layer of leaves and twigs, scent posts marked with urine (often seen only in winter when urine sprays over onto snow); long cylindrical scat, contains hair and bones

Activity: nocturnal, crepuscular; often rests during the day on a tree branch or under a fallen tree or rock ledge

Tracks: forepaw and hind paw 3-4" (7.5-10 cm), round, lobed heel pad, toes spread evenly apart, lacking claw marks; straight line of tracks; hind paws fall near or directly on fore prints (direct register) when walking, often obliterating the forepaw tracks, 12-16" (30-40 cm) stride

Stan's Notes: This wildcat is listed as endangered in the state. Lives in coniferous forests in the central mountains of Colorado. Adults are secretive and rarely seen. Young are not as cautious and are the ones usually seen during the day or near humans.

ear tufts

ruffs

The Canada Lynx is well suited for living in snow. It has large, round furry feet and long legs, which allow it to move quickly through deep snow. Its extra thick fur enables it to stalk silently. The extremely long ear tufts may serve as antennae by detecting vibrations. Will also hunt from trees by dropping onto prey. Can travel 5-7 miles (8-11 km) per night in search of food, mainly Snowshoe Hares (pg. 195) and Ruffed Grouse.

Solitary except to mate and mother its young. Not afraid of water, unlike most cats.

Populations increase and decrease in 10-year cycles, depending on the populations of prey (predator-prey relationship). During peaks in population, ranges expand farther south. Lynx define range by scent marking key spots with urine, often on trees or shrubs near the edges of territory. The male has a larger home range than the female.

Kittens remain with the mother until about 1 year of age. Unlike adults, the young usually bury their scat.

Mountain Lion
Puma concolor

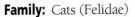

Family: Cats (Felidae)

Size: L 5-6' (1.5-1.8 m); T 2-3' (61-91 cm); H 2½-3' (76-91 cm)

Weight: M 80-267 lb. (36-120 kg); F 64-142 lb. (29-64 kg)

Description: Overall light to tawny brown with light gray-to-white underside. White upper lip and chin, pink nose, dark spot at base of white whiskers. Small oval ears. Long legs. Large round feet. Long rope-like tail with a dark tip.

Origin/Age: native; 10-20 years

Compare: Larger than Canada Lynx (pg. 295), which has a very short tail and long black ear tufts. Bobcat (pg. 291) is much smaller, with a short tail. Look for a long rope-like tail to identify Mountain Lion.

Habitat: river valleys, woodlands, unpopulated locations above 7,000' (2,135 m) in elevation

Home: den, often a sheltered rock crevice, thicket, cave or other protected place; female uses den only to give birth, male does not use den

Food: carnivore; small to large mammals such as hares, rabbits, opossums, raccoons, skunks and deer

Sounds: purrs when content or with cubs, growls, snarls and hisses when threatened or in defense, loud frightening scream during mating, rarely roars

Breeding: year-round mating; 90-100 days gestation

Young: 1-6 (usually 3) cubs once every 2 years; born helpless and blind, covered with dark spots until 3 months, leaves den at 40-70 days and does not return, remains with mother until 15 months

299

stalking

cubs

scat

Signs: long scratches and gashes above 5' (1.5 m) on larger tree trunks, small piles of urine-soaked dirt and debris (serving as scent posts), caches of uneaten prey covered with small branches and leaves; large cylindrical scat up to 10" (25 cm) long and 2" (5 cm) wide, contains hair and bones, sometimes lightly covered with dirt

Activity: primarily nocturnal, to a lesser extent crepuscular; active all year, usually rests in a tree in daytime, rests near a recent kill

Tracks: forepaw and hind paw 5-6" (13-15 cm), round, lobed heel pad, toes evenly spread, lacks claw marks; straight line of tracks; hind paws fall near or onto fore prints (direct register) when walking, often obliterating the forepaw tracks, 12-28" (30-71 cm) stride

Stan's Notes: The Mountain Lion was the most widely ranging cat in the New World in the early 1800s, from Canada to the tip of South America. It was hunted by government professionals to protect livestock from attack until the 1960s. Now seen only in scattered places, often in remote unpopulated areas of western Colorado. Usually secretive and avoids humans, but has been known to attack people. Listed as a big game species in the state.

Contrary to the popular belief that it harms the deer population, it usually hunts and kills only about once each week, feeding for many days on the same kill. It hunts by stalking and springing from cover or dropping from a tree. Frequently drags its kill to a secluded area to eat, buries the carcass and returns to feed over the next couple days, often at night. It is an excellent climber and can leap distances up to 20 feet (6.1 m). Will swim if necessary.

Some people mistakenly think this cat will make a good pet and do not know what to do when their "pet" starts to knock down family members and bite them. These "pets" are released and then often turn up in suburban areas. Usually these are the animals that attack people since they have lost their fear of humans.

Home range of the male is 54-115 square miles (140-299 sq. km) and excludes other male mountain lions. Female range is nearly half the size of the male territory.

Solitary animal except for mating. During that time, the male accompanies the female for up to a couple weeks, traveling and sleeping with her. The female matures sexually at 2-3 years. Only the female raises the young.

male

Pronghorn
Antilocapra americana

Family: Pronghorn (Antilocapridae)

Size: L 4-4½' (1.2-1.4 m); T 3-7" (7.5-18 cm); H 3-3½' (1-1.1 m)

Weight: M 100-140 lb. (45-63 kg); F 75-100 lb. (34-45 kg)

Description: Neck, back and outer legs are light tan to reddish tan. White patches on chin, neck, chest, sides and rump. Ears are trimmed in black. Male horns are 12-20" (30-50 cm) long, black, each with a single point curving inward and small tine about halfway up. Female horns are 3-4" (7.5-10 cm) long, black, each with 1 point and lacking a tine.

Origin/Age: native; 5-10 years

Compare: Smaller than White-tailed Deer (pg. 323), which lacks the white sides and black horns.

Habitat: prairies, grasslands, farmlands, ranches, semi-deserts, elevations below 6,000' (1,830 m)

Home: no den or nest; rests in open terrain, does not seek shelter to give birth or escape bad weather

Food: herbivore; grasses and other green plants

Sounds: usually quiet, snorts loudly to show aggression toward another Pronghorn

Breeding: Sep-Oct mating; 7-8 months gestation; implantation delayed until 1 month after mating

Young: 2 offspring once per year in May or June; 3-13 lb. (1.4-5.9 kg), can walk within minutes of birth, grayer than adult, acquires adult coloration at about 1 month

female

scat

Signs: oval depressions in snow or leaves are evidence of beds; scat in groups of small oval pellets when it has eaten woody material, masses of large segmented scat when it has fed upon green plants

Activity: diurnal, nocturnal; often seen grazing in large open fields, grasslands and prairies

Tracks: front hoof 3" (7.5 cm) long, hind hoof slightly smaller, both with a split heart shape with the point in the front; neat line of single tracks; hind hooves fall near or directly onto fore prints (direct register) when walking, often obliterating the front hoof tracks, heart shape widens when walking in mud or running

Stan's Notes: The fastest land animal in North America. Achieves speeds of up to 70 mph (113 km/h) for short distances, with a cruising speed of 30-40 mph (48-64 km/h). Will simply outrun a predator such as a wolf. Can leap approximately 20 feet (6.1 m) horizontally while running, but is reluctant to jump a standard-height barbed wire fence, choosing to crawl underneath it or pass through between the strands.

Also known as the American Antelope, even though it is not an antelope. The common name "Pronghorn" comes from the small tine or prong located halfway up the horns of the male (buck). It has true horns, which are made of hair-like (keratin) sheaths over bony cores, as opposed to antlers. The only horned animal that sheds horns. Horns are shed annually, usually in November or December after the rut. Shed horns break down quickly in the environment and are rarely found. About one-third of females (does) lack horns.

Eyesight is said to be eight times better than human sight. Able to spot predators approaching from long distances. Well suited to life on the open prairie, with herds traveling great distances to find good grazing areas. Can tolerate cold, but not deep snow.

The buck will gather a harem and start to defend territory during March. If trapped, a buck will fall back behind the herd and fight off the predator with its horns and by kicking.

The doe becomes sexually mature at 16 months. A doe usually produces only one offspring per year for the first couple of years, while an older female will often have twins or sometimes triplets.

Babies spend their first week or so hiding in tall grass, with their mother returning regularly to nurse. The young can outrun most predators at about 1 week of age.

Mountain Goat
Oreamnos americanus

Family: Goats, Sheep and Cattle (Bovidae)

Size: L 4-5' (1.2-1.5 m); T 3-8" (7.5-20 cm); H 3-4½' (1-1.4 m)

Weight: M 150-180 lb. (68-81 kg); F 100-150 lb. (45-68 kg)

Description: All white (sometimes yellowish). Large thick body. Slightly humped shoulders. Distinctive beard, up to 6" (15 cm) long. Backward curving, non-branching black horns. Short pointed ears. Black hooves, nose and eyes. In winter, long shaggy fur covers most of the legs. In summer, smooth and clean-looking with clearly visible legs.

Origin/Age: native; 5-12 years

Compare: Bighorn Sheep (pg. 311) is slightly larger, tan in color and lacks a beard. Look for the white fur of the Mountain Goat to help identify.

Habitat: mountains, rocky cliffs, elevations above 10,000' (3,050 m)

Home: no den or nest; rests in open terrain, does not seek shelter to give birth or escape bad weather

Food: herbivore; grasses and other green plants

Sounds: usually quiet, gives a typical goat-like call

Breeding: Nov-Dec mating; 6 months gestation

Young: 1 (sometimes 2) offspring once per year in May or June; able to walk within minutes of birth, grayer than adult, acquires adult coloration at about 1 month

young

Signs: oval depressions in snow or grass are evidence of beds; scat in groups of small oval pellets when it has eaten dried woody plants, masses of large segmented scat when it has fed upon green plants

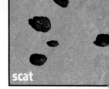

scat

Activity: diurnal, nocturnal; seen grazing on high windswept mountainsides and valleys

Tracks: front hoof 2½-3" (6-7.5 cm) long, hind hoof slightly smaller, widely split at the front, heart shape with the point in the front; neat line of single tracks; hind hooves fall near or directly onto fore prints (direct register) when walking, often obliterating the front hoof tracks, heart shape widens when walking in mud or running

Stan's Notes: This is a hardy animal of high mountaintops and windswept mountain valleys. Eats plants, but seeks exposed earth, where it licks soil for minerals such as salt. Generally sedentary, not moving very far, even for migration. Moves down to the tree line during winter for some shelter.

A thick-bodied large animal with shaggy, woolly fur, which suits it well for the cold, snowy environments in which it lives. During warm summer days it cools off by laying on snow fields. In colder weather it stretches out on sun-warmed rocks. Instead of getting wet to bathe in such harsh environments, it frequently takes dust baths, which keep the coat in good condition.

Hooves have a sharp outer sheath with a soft center, enabling the animal to move across rocky surfaces with ease. Traverses steep cliffs all the time, but accidents do occur, which usually result in death or severe injury.

Often in small herds of less than 50 individuals. Fights between rival males is uncommon, but during breeding season males will assume a threatening posture. Polygamous breeders, males tend females until they come into estrus, which lasts only 48-72 hours. A female does not breed until 3 years of age. Usually has only one offspring. Twins occur less than 30 percent of the time.

Has been introduced into many different areas, including parts of Colorado. All populations in the state result from introductions made over many years starting in the late 1940s, most from Idaho.

male

Bighorn Sheep
Ovis canadensis

Family: Goats, Sheep and Cattle (Bovidae)

Size: L 4-6' (1.2-1.8 m); T 3-6" (7.5-15 cm); H 2½-3½' (76-107 cm)

Weight: M 150-320 lb. (68-144 kg); F 100-200 lb. (45-90 kg)

Description: Stocky and muscular, with a thick neck. Overall light tan to brown with a white rump. Short dark tail. White-tipped muzzle. Extremely large horns, curled, heavily ridged, pointing forward. Female is overall tan to brown with a thin neck, short legs, short oval ears and short, backward curving horns. Coloring of both sexes varies seasonally.

Origin/Age: native; 10-15 years

Compare: Mountain Goat (pg. 307) has a beard, white fur and black horns. Look for the large, distinctive curled horns of the male or the short tan-colored horns of the female to help identify the Bighorn.

Habitat: mountains, rocky cliffs, coniferous and deciduous forests, valleys, elevations above 7,500' (2,285 m)

Home: no den or nest; rests in open terrain, does not seek shelter to give birth or escape bad weather

Food: herbivore; grasses and other green plants, shrubs and other woody plants

Sounds: usually quiet

Breeding: Nov-Dec mating; 6 months gestation

Young: 1 lamb once per year in May or June; can walk within minutes of birth, nurses for several weeks, eats forage at 2 weeks, weaned at 5-6 months

female

Signs: oval depressions in snow or grass are evidence of beds; scat in single round pellets when it has eaten dried woody plants, masses of large segmented scat when it has fed upon green plants

scat

Activity: diurnal; feeds for up to several hours, sits down to rest for up to 2 hours, then feeds again

Tracks: front hoof 2½-3" (6-7.5 cm) long, hind hoof slightly smaller, widely split at the front with a point in the front; neat line of single tracks; hind hooves fall near or directly onto fore prints (direct register) when walking, often obliterating the front hoof tracks, widens when walking in mud, snow or running

Stan's Notes: The official state animal in Colorado, exemplifying the Rocky Mountains. Frequently thought of as an animal of high mountains and steep canyons, but evidence shows that this may be a function imposed by humans due to hunting pressures. Historically it ranged out into the foothills and eastern plains.

Sometimes called Mountain Sheep or Bighorns. The adult male (ram) has massive, heavily ridged horns that can be useful in determining the age of the individual. Horns sweep back and outward, then forward, curving upward, eventually forming what is known as a full curl. Tips of horns are often torn or broken, a condition called brooming. Rams with full curl horns are 7-8 years of age. Horns of younger rams are shorter and more slender.

A gregarious and social animal, with females (ewes) and young (lambs) forming large herds that travel, feed and play together. Older rams form small bachelor herds.

Rams don't breed until 7-8 years of age, when they have full curl horns, with horn size determining the breeding status. The most dominant ram will do most of the breeding of the ewe herd. Ewes breed at 2-3 years of age.

Rams are well known for butting their heads during the rut. They will charge each other at speeds up to 20 mph (32 km/h), crashing their bony foreheads together, resulting in a very loud crack that can be heard from more than a mile away.

Hooves have a hard bony edge and soft spongy center, allowing the animal to scamper over rocky surfaces with ease. Makes short, seasonal migrations from summer to winter ranges.

male

American Bison
Bison bison

RARE

Family: Goats, Sheep and Cattle (Bovidae)

Size: L 8-12' (2.4-3.7 m); T 12-19" (30-48 cm); H 5-6' (1.5-1.8 m)

Weight: M 1,000-2,000 lb. (450-900 kg); F 800-1,000 lb. (360-450 kg)

Description: Dark brown head, lighter brown body and large humped shoulders. Bearded with a long shaggy mane over head and shoulders. Long tuft-tipped tail. Both sexes have short curved horns, which are not shed.

Origin/Age: native; 20-25 years

Compare: A massive animal, hard to confuse with any other. No longer roams freely in Colorado. Rarely seen beyond established areas in parks and farms.

Habitat: prairies, farmlands, open forests

Home: does not use a den or nest, even in bad weather or winter; beds in a different spot each night, rests in the open, laying on the ground or in snow during winter

Food: herbivore; grasses and other green plants, lichens

Sounds: often quiet; male bellows during the rut, female snorts, young bawls for mother's attention

Breeding: Jul-Aug mating; 9-10 months gestation

Young: 1 calf every 1-2 years in May or June; born with reddish brown fur, stands within 30 minutes, walks within hours of its birth, joins herd at 2-3 days, acquires hump, horns and adult coloration at 2-3 months, weaned at 6-7 months

flehmening **female**

scat

Signs: saucer-like depressions in dirt (wallows), 8-10' (2.4-3 m) wide, trees and shrubs with the bark rubbed off, shallow depressions in the snow are evidence of bison beds; scat is similar to that of the domestic cow, flat round patties, 12-14" (30-36 cm) wide

Activity: crepuscular; often rests during the day to chew its cud

Tracks: front hoof 6-7" (15-18 cm) long, hind hoof slightly smaller, both with opposing crescents and more pointed in the front; hind hooves fall behind and slightly to the side of fore prints; crescents widen when walking in mud or running

Stan's Notes: The largest land mammal in North America and considered iconic to the New World. Sometimes called Buffalo, but not related to the Old World buffalo. Historically ranged across Colorado, at one time numbering in the tens of millions. Hunted to near extinction around 1830, when a government policy advocated extermination. There were no bison left in Colorado by 1880 and fewer than 1,000 individuals remained in the United States by the early 1900s. Population restoration started shortly thereafter. While bison are considered extirpated in the state (locally extinct), today some exist in managed herds in Colorado parks and ranches.

Centuries ago, great herds would migrate long distances between winter and summer grounds. Seen in many parts of America today, but no longer migrates. Gregarious, gathering in large herds of nearly 100 individuals, mainly females (cows) and calves.

Uses its massive head and extremely powerful neck muscles to push aside deep snow during winter to feed on the brown grass below. Rolls and rubs its body in wallows to relieve insect bites.

The male (bull) is usually on its own or in a small group during autumn and winter. A dominant bull will join a maternal herd late in summer, just before the rut. Cows that are 2-3 years and older have reached sexual maturity and are fertile for about 24 hours. A bull will curl its upper lip and extend its neck (flehmening) when around cows, perhaps to detect estrus. Bulls "tend" cows that are entering estrus rather than maintaining harems. Competing bulls will strut near each other, showing off their large profile. Mature bulls sometimes face each other, charge, crash together headfirst and use their massive necks to push each other. Fights rarely result in an injury, but occasionally hooking or goring occurs.

sparring

317

Feral Pig
Sus scrofa

Family: Old World Swine (Suidae)

Size: L 4-6' (1.2-1.8 m); T 6-12" (15-30 cm); H 2-3' (61-91 cm)

Weight: M 200-400 lb. (90-180 kg); F 75-300 lb. (34-135 kg)

Description: Extremely variable in color from dark brown and black to gray and white. Large thick body, long pointed snout and short dark legs. Thick fur and well-furred ears. Tail is furred and hangs straight down. Tusks up to 9" (22.5 cm) long, curling out alongside of mouth. Tiny dark eyes. Female has the same colors, but is smaller and lacks tusks.

Origin/Age: non-native; 15-20 years

Compare: Hard to confuse with any animal except domestic pigs, which lack dark fur and have a coiled tail.

Habitat: open forests, shrublands, semideserts, elevations below 5,000' (1,525 m)

Home: no den or nest, rests out in the open or in open forests; female does not seek shelter to give birth, but makes a bed for birthing, never far from water

Food: omnivore; grasses and other green plants, insects, mammals, reptiles, amphibians, birds

Sounds: snorts and grunts similar to domestic pigs

Breeding: year-round mating; 16 weeks gestation

Young: 5-7 piglets twice per year; only 6-8" (15-20 cm) at birth, usually brown with pale longitudinal body stripes, able to walk and follow mother at 1 week, nurses for 3 months

Signs: large holes in the ground where plants, crops, fences, posts or other objects were uprooted, mud wallowing holes; mass of pellets or tubular segments, usually near uprooted plants

Activity: diurnal, nocturnal, crepuscular; feeds for up to several hours, sits down to rest for up to 2 hours, then feeds again

Tracks: front hoof 2½-3" (6-7.5 cm) long, hind hoof slightly smaller, widely split at the front with a point in front; neat line of paired tracks, slightly offset; hind hooves fall near fore prints (no direct register) when walking

Stan's Notes: Most Feral Pigs are descendants of European wild hogs that were introduced into the United States for food or for sporting purposes. Some are the progeny of escaped domestic swine that became feral over just a couple generations. Now found in over half of the states, mainly in the South, with range expanding northward. Feral Pigs prefer forests that produce acorn crops, but in absence of this they will live in open shrublands and other areas not far from water.

The presence of Feral Pigs has a very noticeable impact on native wildlife and plant life, as well as on crops and livestock, and for this reason the animals are not welcome in many areas. Other areas, however, embrace their presence with managed hunting.

Also known as the Wild Hog, Wild Boar, Russian Wild Boar or Razorback. Like domestic swine, Feral Pigs have a cartilaginous, flexible snout.

A female (sow) and her young (piglets) will feed together and sometimes join other groups in herds of up to 35 individuals. The male (boar) tends to be solitary unless it is breeding season. Boars will fight, using their tusks to determine dominance and the right to breed.

Piglets stay with their mother for a year. They are usually brown with pale longitudinal body stripes at birth, and become sexually mature at just 18 months of age.

male

White-tailed Deer
Odocoileus virginianus

Family: Deer (Cervidae)

Size: L 4-7' (1.2-2.1 m); T 6-12" (15-30 cm); H 3-4' (1-1.2 m)

Weight: M 100-300 lb. (45-135 kg); F 75-200 lb. (34-90 kg)

Description: Reddish brown during summer, grayish brown during winter. Large ears, white inside with black edges. A white eye-ring, nose band, chin, throat and belly. Brown tail with a black tip and white underside. Male has antlers with many tines and an antler spread of 12-36" (30-91 cm). Female has a thinner neck than male and lacks antlers.

Origin/Age: native; 5-10 years

Compare: Slightly smaller than the much more common Mule Deer (pg. 327), which has a small, thin white tail with a black tip. The Elk (pg. 335) is more than twice the size and weight of White-tailed Deer and has a dark mane.

Habitat: all habitats, all elevations

Home: no den or nest; sleeps in a different spot every night, beds may be concentrated in one area, does not use a shelter in bad weather or winter, will move to a semisheltered area (yard) with a good supply of food in winter

Food: herbivore; grasses and other green plants, acorns and nuts in summer, twigs and buds in winter

Sounds: loud whistle-like snorts, male grunts, fawn bleats

Breeding: late Oct-Nov mating; 6-7 months gestation

Young: 1-2 fawns once per year in May or June; covered with white spots, walks within hours of birth

323

young male

tree rub

female

scat

Signs: browsed twigs that are ripped or torn (due to the lack of upper incisor teeth), tree rubs (saplings scraped or stripped of bark) made by male while polishing antlers during the rut, oval depressions in snow or leaves are evidence of beds; round, hard brown pellets during winter, segmented cylindrical masses of scat in spring and summer

Activity: nocturnal, crepuscular; often moves along same trails to visit feeding areas, moves around less when snow is deep

Tracks: front hoof 2-3" (5-7.5 cm) long, hind hoof slightly smaller, both with a split heart shape with the point in the front; neat line of single tracks; hind hooves fall near or directly onto fore prints (direct register) when walking

Stan's Notes: Also known as Virginia Deer or Whitetail. Almost extirpated in the 1920s, it has recovered well and is now found in most river bottoms throughout the eastern half of Colorado.

fawn

Much longer guard hairs in winter give the animal a larger appearance than in summer. Individual hairs of the winter coat are thick and hollow and provide excellent insulation. Falling snow often does not melt on its back.

In summer, antlers are covered with a furry skin called velvet. Velvet contains a network of blood vessels that supplies nutrients to the growing antlers. New antler growth begins after the male (buck) drops his antlers in January or February. Some females (does) have been known to grow antlers.

Deer are dependent on the location of the food supply. In winter large groups move to low moist areas (yards) that have plenty of food. This yarding behavior helps keep trails open and provides some protection from predators. Eats 5-9 pounds (2.3-4.1 kg) of food per day, preferring acorns in fall and fresh grass in spring. Its four-chambered stomach enables the animal to get nutrients from poor food sources, such as twigs, and eat and drink substances that are unsuitable for humans.

Able to run up to 37 mph (60 km/h), jump up to 8½ feet (2.6 m) high and leap 30 feet (9.1 m). Also an excellent swimmer.

The buck is solitary in spring and early summer, but seeks other bucks in late summer and early fall to spar. Bucks are polygamous. The largest, most dominant bucks mate with many does.

For a couple weeks after birth, fawns lay still all day while their mother is away feeding. Mother nurses them evenings and nights.

mâle

Mule Deer
Odocoileus hemionus

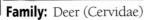

Family: Deer (Cervidae)

Size: L 4-7½' (1.2-2.3 m); T 4-9" (10-22.5 cm); H 3½-4' (1.1-1.2 m)

Weight: M 100-475 lb. (45-214 kg); F 75-160 lb. (34-72 kg)

Description: Reddish brown in summer. Gray in winter. White chin, throat and rump. Large ears, white inside with black tips and edges. A thin white tail with a black tip. Male has large antlers with 2 main beams, many tines and an antler spread of 24-48" (61-122 cm). Female is 20 percent smaller than male, has a thinner neck and lacks antlers.

Origin/Age: native; 10-15 years

Compare: Stockier and slightly larger than the much less common White-tailed Deer (pg. 323), which has a larger, wider tail. Antlers on White-tailed Deer have only 1 main beam. Mule Deer runs with its tail down, while the White-tailed Deer runs with its tail raised and waving back and forth.

Habitat: prairies, fields, farmlands, forests, all elevations

Home: no den or nest; doesn't use shelter in bad weather or winter, sleeps in dense cover each night

Food: herbivore; grasses and other green plants, acorns and nuts in summer, twigs and buds in winter

Sounds: generally quiet, male will grunt, fawn will bleat when it calls to its mother

Breeding: late Nov-Dec mating; 6-7 months gestation

Young: 1-2 fawns once per year in May or June; covered with white spots, walks within hours of birth

young male

fawn

female

Signs: ripped or torn browsed twigs (due to the lack of upper incisor teeth), oval depressions in snow or leaves are evidence of beds; segmented cylindrical masses of scat in spring and summer, round, hard brown pellets during winter

scat

Activity: nocturnal, crepuscular; will wander about seeking feeding areas where snow is gone, exposing grass

Tracks: front hoof 2½-3¼" (6-8 cm) long, hind hoof slightly smaller, both with a split heart shape with the point in the front; neat line of single tracks; hind hooves fall near or directly onto fore prints (direct register) when walking, fore hooves fall in front of hind prints when bounding in a distinctive gait (stotting)

Stan's Notes: A common resident throughout Colorado in all ecosystems. Also called Black-tailed Deer due to its black-tipped tail. Common name "Mule" comes from its large mule-like ears, which can move independently to focus on sounds coming from two different directions simultaneously. Although the ears appear substantially larger than those of White-tailed Deer (pg. 323), measurements confirm they are about the same in both species.

Mule Deer have a unique, stiff-legged bounding gait called stotting, in which the front and hind legs move in the same fashion at the same time. Stotting helps to positively identify this animal since White-tailed Deer do not do this.

The male (buck) drops its antlers in January or February, with new growth beginning immediately. Growing antlers are covered with a velvety covering that contains a network of blood vessels. Each successive set of antlers gets larger until a buck reaches peak maturity at 6-7 years. Antlers grown after that age range have an irregular growth pattern, resulting in atypically shaped antlers. Antler growth is also affected by the amount and quality of food available. Bucks are solitary until just before the rut, when several may come together to look for females (does). Sparring between bucks is common. The objective is to overpower the opponent, and injury rarely results. Highly polygamous, a dominant buck will mate with nearly all does in his area.

Does remain in small to large groups year-round. A doe may mate with more than one buck per season. Younger does will produce single fawns, while older does produce twins annually. Fawns remain hidden in tall vegetation for their first month. Mothers visit their young each evening to nurse.

male

Moose
Alces alces

Family: Deer (Cervidae)

Size: L 7-9' (2.1-2.7 m); T 4-7" (10-18 cm); H 6½-7½' (2-2.3 m)

Weight: M 900-1,400 lb. (405-630 kg); F 700-1,100 lb. (315-495 kg)

Description: Dark reddish brown fur, lighter brown in winter. Large light brown ears. Bulbous muzzle, usually darker than head. Obvious hump at shoulders. Nearly black belly and legs. Small brown tail. Male has a flap of skin hanging underneath the chin (dewlap), flattened (palmate) antlers with multiple points and an antler spread of 4-5' (1.2-1.5 m). Female is much smaller than male and lacks the dewlap and antlers.

Origin/Age: native; 15-20 years

Compare: Hard to misidentify this extremely large animal.

Habitat: mixed or coniferous forests, wetlands, elevations up to 10,000' (3,050 m)

Home: no den or nest; bed in a different spot each night, possibly in one area, moves to a semisheltered area (yard) with a good supply of food in winter

Food: herbivore; aquatic vegetation, grasses and other green plants, acorns, nuts, twigs, buds

Sounds: during the rut, male bellows loudly, grunts and groans, female gives long moans

Breeding: late Sep-Nov mating; 8 months gestation

Young: 1-2 (usually 1) calves in spring; light brown fur, lacks spots, stands and walks within 24 hours, swims at about 7 days

flehmening

shedding velvet

tree rub

mother and calf

summer scat

winter scat

Signs: tree rubs (saplings scraped or stripped of bark), made by the male while polishing antlers during the rut, browsed twigs that are ripped or torn, depressions in the ground (scrapes) up to 4' (1.2 m) wide, often muddy with a strong smell of urine; segmented cylindrical masses of scat in spring and summer, frequently green to nearly black, large brown pellets in winter, usually round and hard

Activity: nocturnal, crepuscular

Tracks: front hoof 5-6" (13-15 cm) long, hind hoof slightly smaller, both with a split heart shape with the point in the front; line of individual tracks; hind hooves fall near or to the side of fore prints; heart shape widens and 2 dots (made by dewclaws) print just behind each heart-shaped print when in mud or snow

Stan's Notes: Only one moose species worldwide, with several subspecies. Name comes from the Algonquian Indian *moos*, which refers to its habit of eating twigs. Historically was an occasional visitor to the state and didn't appear to be breeding. Introduced by the Colorado Division of Wildlife in 1978. Several sustainable populations now exist in the central mountains. Found in cooler regions due to its stomach (which produces heat by fermentation), its inability to perspire and its large size. Easily stressed by heat.

The function of the flap of skin under the male's neck (dewlap) is unknown. Poor vision, but excellent hearing and the ability to smell food underneath snow. Has a four-chambered stomach for processing woody plants. Able to eat up to 45 pounds (20.3 kg) of vegetation per day. An extremely quiet animal while feeding in woods. May appear slow and gangly, but can run up to 35 mph (56 km/h) and swim up to 6 mph (10 km/h) for long periods. Spends much of its time in water, eating aquatic plants, taking refuge from biting insects and heat.

The male (bull) is solitary in summer and seeks breeding females (cows) in fall. Matures sexually before 5-7 years, but is not large enough to compete with dominant bulls for cows until after 5-7 years. Reaches prime condition at 7-12 years. Visually attuned to an opponent's antlers, it will spar with other bulls, usually those with a similar antler size, to assert dominance and to determine which will mate with available cows. Often seen curling its upper lip back while extending its neck (flehmening) when around cows. The lip curl is thought to enhance the sense of smell and allow the bull to detect when a cow is in estrus. Cows group together in winter where food is available and snow is packed down, which makes walking easier.

A wandering moose will often make the local news when sighted in urban areas. This behavior is often the result of a fatal disorder caused by a worm in the brain. An afflicted moose will wander in a straight line for hundreds of miles.

male

Elk
Cervus canadensis

Family: Deer (Cervidae)

Size: L 7-9½' (2.1-2.9 m); T 3-8" (7.5-20 cm); H 4½-5' (1.4-1.5 m)

Weight: M 600-1,100 lb. (270-495 kg); F 450-650 lb. (203-293 kg)

Description: Brown to tan with a darker head, neck, belly and legs. Rump patch is light tan to yellowish. Short stubby tail. Male has large antlers with many tines and an antler spread of 4-5' (1.2-1.5 m). Female has a lighter mane than male, a thinner neck and lacks antlers.

Origin/Age: native; 15-20 years

Compare: Smaller than Moose (pg. 331), which is darker brown and lacks a light rump patch. More than twice the size and weight of its cousin, the White-tailed Deer (pg. 323), which lacks the dark mane.

Habitat: mixed forests, fields, farmlands, prairies, elevations above 6,000' (1,830 m)

Home: no den or nest; rests out in the open on the ground, will bed in a different area each night

Food: herbivore; grasses and other green plants

Sounds: snorts and grunts, male gives a bugle call or high-pitched whistle to challenge other males during rut; call can be heard up to several miles away

Breeding: late Aug-Nov mating; 9 months gestation

Young: 1-2 calves once per year in June or July; covered with spots until about 3 months, feeds solely by nursing for the first 30 days, weaned at 9 month

bugling

sparring

female

summer scat

winter scat

Signs: tree rubs (saplings scraped or stripped of bark) made by the male while polishing antlers during rut, ground scrapes (shallow depressions in the ground) made by male hooves to attract females and where male urinates and defecates, shallow depressions in snow made from resting

Activity: nocturnal, crepuscular; can be seen during the day walking and feeding

Tracks: front hoof 4-4½" (10-11 cm) long, hind hoof slightly smaller, both with a split heart shape with the point in the front; line of individual tracks; hind hooves fall near or onto fore prints (direct register) when walking, often obliterating the front hoof tracks; heart shape widens and 2 dots (made by dewclaws) print just behind each heart-shaped print when in mud or snow

Stan's Notes: There is only one species of elk in North America, but there are four subspecies. Sometimes called Wapiti, which is a Shawnee Indian word meaning "pale deer." The British name for the moose is "Elk." This name apparently was misapplied by our early settlers and has remained since.

Once widespread in the western half of Colorado, this mammal almost disappeared from the state, dwindling down to 500-600 individuals by the early 1900s due to overhunting. Now seen in a couple areas of the state with dramatically increased populations due to the lack of natural predators such as the wolf.

A highly gregarious animal. Most herds consist of many females (cows) and calves. Highly territorial, marking the edges of its area with a scent secreted from glands on the sides of its chin and muzzle. Makes a shallow, saucer-like depression in dirt (wallow) in which it rolls, coating its fur with dust to help protect against annoying insects. It is a fast animal, with males (bulls) capable of reaching 35 mph (56 km/h) for short distances. Also a strong swimmer that will wade across nearly any river or stream.

A bull is solitary or found in small groups, but will join the herd during the rut. Bulls are capable of breeding at 2 years. However, rarely is a bull large enough at that age to fight off older males and establish a harem. Will thrash small trees to polish its antlers. Tears up vegetation and wears it on antlers to express dominance. Top bulls challenge each other by clashing their antlers together in a jousting fashion. Rarely do these fights result in any injury or death. The most polygamous animal in America, one bull will mate with all cows in the harem.

The cow becomes sexually mature at 3 years. A cow will leave the herd to give birth, rejoining the group 4-10 days later.

Black Bear
Ursus americanus

Family: Bears (Ursidae)

Size: L 4½-6' (1.4-1.8 m); T 3-7" (7.5-18 cm); H 3-3½' (1-1.1 m)

Weight: M 100-900 lb. (45-405 kg); F 90-525 lb. (41-236 kg)

Description: Nearly all black, sometimes brown, tan or cinnamon. Short round ears. Light brown snout. May have a small white patch on its chest. Short tail, which often goes unnoticed.

Origin/Age: native; 15-30 years

Compare: Much smaller than the Grizzly Bear (pg. 343), which is extremely rare in Colorado.

Habitat: forests, wetlands, prairies, elevations above 6,000' (1,830 m)

Home: den, underneath a fallen tree or in a rock crevice or cave, may dig a den 5-6' (1.5-1.8 m) deep with a small cavity at the end; male sometimes hibernates on the ground without shelter

Food: omnivore; leaves, nuts, roots, fruit, berries, grass, insects, fish, small mammals, carrion

Sounds: huffs, puffs or grunts and groans when walking, loud snorts made by air forced from nostrils, loud roars when fighting and occasionally when mating, motor-like humming when content

Breeding: Jun-Jul mating; 60-90 days gestation; implantation delayed until November after mating

Young: 1-5 (usually 2) cubs once every other year in January or February; born covered with fine d fur, weighing only ½-1 lb. (.2-.5 kg)

claw marks

brown morph

scat

Signs: series of long narrow scars on tree trunks, usually as high as the bear can reach, made by scratching and biting, rub marks with snagged hair on the lower part of tree trunks or on large rocks, made by rubbing and scratching when shedding its winter coat; large dark cylindrical scat or piles of loose scat, usually contains berries and nuts, may contain animal hair, undigested plant stems and roots

Activity: diurnal, nocturnal; often seen feeding during the day

Tracks: hind paw 7-9" (18-22.5 cm) long, 5" (13 cm) wide with 5 toes, turns inward slightly, looks like a human track, forepaw 4" (10 cm) long, 5" (13 cm) wide with 5 toes, claw marks on all ⌐et; fore and hind prints are parallel, hind paws fall several ⌐es in front of fore prints; shuffles feet when walking

Stan's Notes: The Black Bear is unique to North America. Has a shuffling gait and frequently appears clumsy. It is not designed for speed, but can run up to 30 mph (48 km/h) for short distances. A powerful swimmer, however, and good at climbing trees. It has color vision, but poor eyesight and relies on smell to find most of its food. Often alone except for mating in early summer or when bears gather at a large food supply such as a garbage dump. Feeds heavily throughout summer, adding layers of fat for hibernation.

Hibernates up to six months per year beginning in late fall. Heart rate drops from 70 to 10-20 beats per minute. Body temperature drops only 1-12°F (-17°C to -11°C), which is not enough to change mental functions. Doesn't eat, drink, pass feces or urinate during hibernation, yet can be roused and will move around in the den. The female can lose up to 40 percent of her body weight during hibernation.

Male has a large territory of up to 15 square miles (39 sq. km) that often encompasses several female territories. Males fight each other for breeding rights and usually have scars from fights. The male bear matures at 3-4 years of age, but doesn't reach full size until 10-12 years. Males do not take part in raising young.

cub

The female bear doesn't breed until it is 2-3 years of age. Females that have more body fat when entering hibernation will have more cubs than females with less fat. If a female does not have enough fat, she will not give birth. Mother bears, which average 177 pounds (80 kg), are approximately 250 times the size of newborns. A short gestation and tiny cubs are the result of the reproductive process during hibernation.

Grizzly Bear
Ursus arctos

Family: Bears (Ursidae)

Size: L 4½-8½' (1.4-2.6 m); T 3-8" (7.5-20 cm); H 4½-5½' (1.4-1.7 m)

Weight: M 500-1,700 lb. (225-765 kg); F 350-1,400 lb. (158-630 kg)

Description: Large all-brown bear, sometimes varying shades of brown to yellow, with silver- or gray-tipped hairs (grizzled) on the back. Pronounced mane of long hairs on shoulders, often another color than the body. Hump at the shoulder region, higher than the rump. Large blocky head, short round ears, tiny eyes and short snout. Huge feet with very large, slightly curved claws, 4" (10 cm) long.

Origin/Age: native; 15-30 years

Compare: The Black Bear (pg. 339) is smaller, much more common and lacks the hump at the shoulders.

Habitat: mountains, rocky cliffs, valleys, along streams, elevations above 7,000' (2,135 m)

Home: den under a large rock, under the roots of a fallen tree in winter, otherwise rests in open terrain

Food: omnivore; mostly green plants; also eats insects, roots, fruit, nuts, pine cones, animals, fish, carrion

Sounds: huffs, puffs, snorts and grunts

Breeding: May-Jun mating; 2-3 months gestation; delayed implantation

Young: 1-4 cubs once every other year in January or February; born fully furred, weighing only 1-3 lb. (.5-1.4 kg), nurses right away, stays with mother for 2 (sometimes 3) years

343

Signs: large oval depressions in snow or grass are evidence of beds; bear trees, with large tooth and claw marks 6-10' (1.8-3 m) high and tufts of hair caught in bark; cylindrical scat, at least 2" (5 cm) wide and up to 6-10" (15-25 cm) long, sometimes with fur and bones evident, masses of large round mounds of scat when it has fed primarily on green plants

Activity: diurnal, nocturnal; can be seen grazing on high windswept mountainsides and in valleys, forests at the tree line

Tracks: hind paw 10-14" (25-36 cm) long, forepaw 6-7" (15-18 cm) long, both 7-8" (18-20 cm) wide with 5 toes and claw marks on all feet; alternating fore and hind prints; can be seen on the same path going back and forth to feeding areas

Stan's Notes: Once common throughout Colorado, now listed as endangered with no known sustainable populations in the state. Occasionally 1-2 individuals show up from neighboring states to the north. A grizzly seen in Colorado should be reported to the Colorado Division of Wildlife.

The grizzly walks with a swaggering gate, swinging its head back and forth. It can run very fast for short distances to overtake prey. Able to climb trees, but not as well as its smaller cousin, the Black Bear (pg. 339). Usually solitary except for mothers with cubs.

A highly intelligent animal with an exceptional sense of smell and hearing. Eyesight is average.

Primarily vegetarian, with grasses and other green plants making up over 90 percent of its diet during summer. Often digs for roots and insects in forested areas. Does well at finding berries and nuts and catching fish. Hunts newborn elk, deer and other hooved animals during spring.

Can put on up to 450 pounds (203 kg) of fat in preparation for winter. Not a true hibernator, waking for short periods of time. Does not eat, drink or defecate for up to 6 months during winter, using stored fat as an energy source. Heart rate and respirations are decreased to conserve energy, but a hibernating grizzly is still very much awake. Females are fully awake during the birth of their cubs and remain active to care for the newborns.

Do not surprise or startle a grizzly. They can be unpredictable and aggressive, and great care should be taken when encountering one of these animals.

Feral Horse
Equus caballus

Family: Horses (Equidae)

Size: L 5-7' (1.5-2.1 m); T 1-2' (30-61 cm); H 4½-5½' (1.4-1.7 m)

Weight: M 800-900 lb. (360-405 kg); F 550-750 lb. (248-338 kg)

Description: Nearly identical to domestic horses in size, shape and color, with many colors and patterns. Large powerful body. Long snout. Long mane and tail. May have faint zebra-like striping on the sides.

Origin/Age: non-native; 20-35 years

Compare: Slightly smaller than domestic horses, otherwise extremely hard to differentiate from afar except for its behavior. The Feral Horse is often skittish, scruffy-looking and has no branding. Look for it in large, remote wild areas and public lands.

Habitat: semideserts, shrublands, valleys, elevations up to 7,500' (2,285 m)

Home: no den or nest; rests in open terrain, does not seek shelter to give birth or escape bad weather

Food: herbivore; grasses and other green plants, shrubs and other woody plants

Sounds: typical horse whinnies, nickers, squeals, neighs and snorts

Breeding: Jun-Aug mating; 11 months gestation

Young: 1 colt once every other year in May or June; can walk within minutes of birth, nurses for several weeks

flehmening

mother and colt

Signs: oval depressions in snow or grass are evidence of beds; scat in piles of large patties, several males will use a common defecation site, resulting in a large formation called a stud pile; large amounts of urine, sometimes pooling on flat open ground

Activity: diurnal; feeds for up to several hours, rests for up to 2 hours, then feeds again, may take a break at midday

Tracks: front and hind hooves 3-5" (7.5-13 cm) wide, each a large single semicircle; wide space between each print; hind hooves do not register in fore prints

Stan's Notes: Horses were domesticated over 5,000 years ago in the Old World and have been introduced all over the world. The Feral Horse, sometimes known as Wild Horse, has a wide variety of colors and patterns. Although it is usually slightly smaller than domestic horses, it is often impossible to distinguish Feral Horses from domesticated horses ranging on public lands.

Diet is 90 percent grass, so the Feral won't be seen far from open grass habitat. Also needs to be near freestanding water. Typically visits a local watering hole at least daily, often in late afternoon.

Social structure is complex. Usually seen in small herds of mostly adult females (mares), their young (colts) and a dominant male (stallion). Individuals seen on their own are usually injured or young stallions who have yet to establish themselves in a herd.

Young stallions are forced out of their herds at age 3 and form small bachelor herds, led by a dominant stallion. Fights between stallions start with threat postures and displays such as laying the ears back, opening the mouth, arching the neck and shaking the head. Physical fights include biting and kicking, often resulting in serious injury.

Takes a dust bath by rolling in exposed soils. Mutual grooming is a daily activity, although a stallion does not groom or allow itself to be groomed.

GLOSSARY

Browse: Twigs, buds and leaves that deer, moose, elk and other animals eat.

Canid: A member of the Wolves, Foxes and Coyote family, which includes dogs.

Carnivore: An animal, such as a mink, fox or wolf, that eats the flesh of other animals for its main nutrition.

Carrion: Dead or decaying flesh. Carrion is a significant food source for many animal species.

Cecum: The large pouch that forms the beginning of the large intestine. Also known as the blind gut.

Cheek ruff: A gathering of long stiff hairs on each side of the face of an animal, ending in a downward point. Seen in bobcats and lynx.

Coprophagy: The act of reingesting fecal pellets. Coprophagy enables rabbits and hares to gain more nourishment since the pellets pass through the digestive system a second time.

Crepuscular: Active during the early morning and late evening hours as opposed to day or night. See *diurnal* and *nocturnal*.

Cud: Food regurgitated from the first stomach to the mouth, and chewed again. Cud is produced by hoofed animals such as deer or bison, which have a four-chambered stomach (ruminants).

Dewclaw: A nonfunctional (vestigial) digit on the feet of some animals, which does not touch the ground. Seen in deer, elk and moose.

Dewlap: A fold of loose skin hanging from the neck of some animals such as moose.

Direct register: The act of a hind paw landing or registering in the track left by a forepaw, resulting in two prints that appear like one track. Usually occurs when walking.

Diurnal: Active during daylight hours as opposed to nighttime hours. Opposite of *nocturnal*.

Drey: The nest of a squirrel.

Duff: The layer of decaying leaves, grasses, twigs or branches, often several inches thick, on a forest floor or prairie.

Echolocation: A sensory system in bats, dolphins and some shrews, in which inaudible, high-pitched sounds are emitted and the returning echoes are interpreted to determine the direction and distance of objects such as prey.

Estrus: A state of sexual readiness in most female animals that immediately precedes ovulation, and the time when females are most receptive to mating. Also known as heat.

Extirpate: To hunt or trap into extinction in a region or state.

Flehmen: The lift of the upper lip and grimace an animal makes when it draws air into its mouth and over its Jacobson's organ, which is thought to help analyze the scents (pheromones) wafting in the air. Frequently seen in cats, deer and bison.

Fossorial: Well suited for burrowing or digging. Describes an animal such as a mole.

Gestation: Pregnancy. The period of development in the uterus of a mammal from conception up to birth.

Grizzled: Streaked or tipped with gray, or partly gray. Describes the appearance of some fur.

Guard hairs: The long outer hairs of an animal's coat, which provide warmth. Guard hairs are typically hollow and usually thicker and darker than the soft hairs underneath.

Haul out: A well-worn trail or area on the shore where an animal, such as an otter, climbs or hauls itself out of the water.

Herbivore: An animal, such as a rabbit, deer, moose or elk, that eats plants for its main nutrition.

Hibernation: A torpid or lethargic state characterized by decreased heart rate, respiration and body temperature, and occurring in close quarters for long periods during winter. See *torpor*.

Hoary: Partly white or silver streaked, or tipped with white or silver. Describes the appearance of some fur.

Hummock: A low mound or ridge of earth or plants.

Insectivore: An animal, such as a shrew, that eats insects as its main nutrition.

Keratin: A hard protein that is the chief component of the hair, nails, horns and hooves of an animal.

Microflora: Bacterial life living in the gut or first stomach of an animal. Microflora help break down food and aid in the digestive process.

Midden: A mound or deposit of pine cone parts and other refuse. A midden is evidence of a favorite feeding site of an animal such as a squirrel.

Morph: One of various distinct shapes, structural differences or colors of an animal. Color morphs do not change during the life of an animal.

Nictitating membrane: A second, inner eyelid, usually translucent, that protects and moistens the eye.

Nocturnal: Active during nighttime hours as opposed to daylight hours. Opposite of *diurnal*.

Nonretractile: That which cannot be drawn back or in. Describes the claws of a dog. Opposite of *retractile*.

Omnivore: An animal, such as a bear, that eats a wide range of foods including plants, insects and the flesh of other animals as its main nutrition.

Patagium: A thin membrane extending from the body to the front and hind limbs, forming a wing-like extension. Seen in flying squirrels and bats.

Population: All individuals of a species within a specific area.

Predator: An animal that hunts, kills and eats other animals. See *prey*.

Prey: An animal that is hunted, killed and eaten by a predator. See *predator*.

Retractile: That which can be drawn back or in. Describes the claws of a cat. Opposite of *nonretractile*.

Rut: An annually recurring condition of sexual readiness and reproductive activity in mammals, such as deer and elk, that usually occurs in autumn. See *estrus*.

Scat: The fecal droppings of an animal.

Scent marking: A means of marking territory, signaling sexual availability or communicating an individual's identity. An animal scent marks with urine, feces or by secreting a tiny amount of odorous liquid from a gland, usually near the base of the tail, chin or feet, onto specific areas such as rocks, trees and stumps.

Semiprehensile: Suited for partially seizing, grasping or holding, especially by wrapping around an object, but not a means of full support. Describes the tail of an opossum.

Stride: In larger animals, the distance between individual tracks. In smaller animals such as weasels, the distance between sets of tracks.

Subnivean: Below the surface of snow, but above the surface of the earth. See *subterranean*.

Subterranean: Below the surface of the earth.

Talus: The accumulation of many rocks at the base of a cliff or mountain slope.

Tannin: A bitter-tasting astringent found in the nuts of many plant species.

Torpor: A torpid or lethargic state resembling hibernation, characterized by decreased heart rate, respiration and body temperature, but usually shorter, lasting from a few hours to several days or weeks. See *hibernation*.

Tragus: A fleshy projection in the central part of the ear of most bats. The size and shape of the tragus may be used to help identify some bat species.

Tree rub: An area on small to medium trees where the bark has been scraped or stripped off. A tree rub is made by a male deer polishing his antlers in preparation for the rut.

Velvet: A soft, furry covering on antlers that contains many blood vessels, which support antler growth. Velvet is shed when antlers reach full size. Seen in the Deer family.

Vibrissae: Sensitive bristles and hairs, such as whiskers, that help an animal feel its way in the dark. Vibrissae are often on the face, legs and tail.

Wallow: A depression in the ground that is devoid of vegetation, where an animal, such as a bison, rolls around on its back to "bathe" in dirt.

HELPFUL RESOURCES

Emergency

For an animal bite, please seek medical attention at an emergency room or call 911. Injured or orphaned animals should be turned over to a licensed wildlife rehabilitator. Check your local listings for a rehabilitator near you.

Web Pages

The internet is a valuable place to learn more about mammals. You may find studying mammals on the net a fun way to discover additional information about them or to spend a long winter night. These websites will assist you in your pursuit of mammals. If a web address doesn't work (they often change a bit), just enter the name of the group into a search engine to track down the new web address.

Site and Address:

Smithsonian Institution - North American Mammals
www.mnh.si.edu/mna

The American Society of Mammalogists
www.mammalsociety.org

National Wildlife Rehabilitators Association
www.nwrawildlife.org

International Wildlife Rehabilitation Council
www.theiwrc.org

Colorado Parks and Wildlife
www.wildlife.state.co.us

Colorado Department of Natural Resources (DNR)
www.dnr.state.co.us

Author Stan Tekiela's home page
www.naturesmart.com

Colorado's Artiodactyla Order

ORDER	SUBORDER	FAMILY	SUBFAMILY

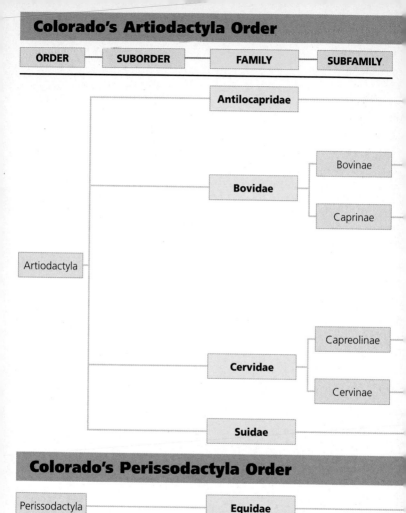

Artiodactyla

- Antilocapridae
- Bovidae
  - Bovinae
  - Caprinae
- Cervidae
  - Capreolinae
  - Cervinae
- Suidae

Colorado's Perissodactyla Order

Perissodactyla — Equidae

Even-toed Hooved Animals

Pronghorn pg. 303
Antilocapra americana

Mountain Goat pg. 307
Oreamnos americanus

American Bison pg. 315
Bison bison

Bighorn Sheep pg. 311
Ovis canadensis

White-tailed Deer pg. 323
Odocoileus virginianus

Mule Deer pg. 327
Odocoileus hemionus

Moose pg. 331
Alces alces

Elk pg. 335
Cervus canadensis

Feral Pig pg. 319
Sus scrofa

Odd-toed Hooved Animals

Feral Horse pg. 347
Equus caballus

Box colors match the
corresponding section of the book.

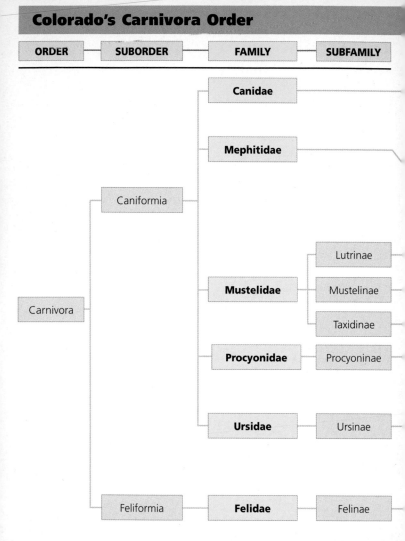

Colorado's Carnivora Order

ORDER	SUBORDER	FAMILY	SUBFAMILY

Carnivora

Caniformia

Canidae

Mephitidae

Mustelidae
- Lutrinae
- Mustelinae
- Taxidinae

Procyonidae — Procyoninae

Ursidae — Ursinae

Feliformia

Felidae — Felinae

Meat-eating Predators

Kit Fox pg. 267
Vulpes macrotis
Swift Fox pg. 271
Vulpes velox
Red Fox pg. 279
Vulpes vulpes

Gray Fox pg. 275
Urocyon cinereoargenteus

Coyote pg. 283
Canis latrans
Gray Wolf pg. 287
Canis lupus

Western Spotted Skunk pg. 239
Spilogale gracilis

Striped Skunk pg. 243
Mephitis mephitis

Northern River Otter pg. 235
Lontra canadensis

Short-tailed Weasel pg. 207
Mustela erminea
Long-tailed Weasel pg. 211
Mustela frenata
Black-footed Ferret pg. 223
Mustela nigripes

American Marten pg. 215
Martes americana

Mink pg. 219
Neovison vison

Wolverine pg. 231
Gulo gulo

American Badger pg. 227
Taxidea taxus

Ringtail pg. 247
Bassariscus astutus

Northern Raccoon pg. 251
Procyon lotor

Black Bear pg. 339
Ursus americanus

Grizzly Bear pg. 343
Ursus arctos

Bobcat pg. 291
Lynx rufus
Canada Lynx pg. 295
Lynx canadensis

Mountain Lion pg. 299
Puma concolor

Box colors match the
corresponding section of the book.

359

Colorado's Chiroptera Order

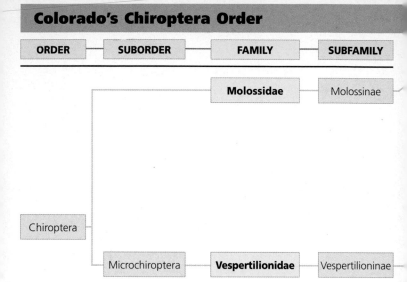

ORDER	SUBORDER	FAMILY	SUBFAMILY
		Molossidae	Molossinae
Chiroptera			
	Microchiroptera	**Vespertilionidae**	Vespertilioninae

Colorado's Didelphimorphia Order

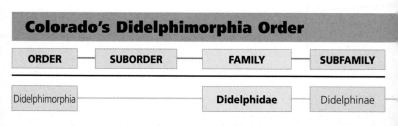

ORDER	SUBORDER	FAMILY	SUBFAMILY
Didelphimorphia		**Didelphidae**	Didelphinae

Bats

Brazilian Free-tailed Bat pg. 90
Tadarida brasiliensis

Big Free-tailed Bat pg. 91
Nyctinomops macrotis

Little Brown Bat pg. 90
Myotis lucifugus
Western Small-footed Myotis pg. 90
Myotis ciliolabrum
Fringed Myotis pg. 90
Myotis thysanodes
California Myotis pg. 91
Myotis californicus
Yuma Myotis pg. 91
Myotis yumanensis
Long-eared Myotis pg. 91
Myotis evotis
Long-legged Myotis pg. 91
Myotis volans
Cave Myotis pg. 91
Myotis velifer

Western Pipistrelle pg. 90
Pipistrellus hesperus

Big Brown Bat pg. 87
Eptesicus fuscus

Red Bat pg. 90
Lasiurus borealis
Hoary Bat pg. 91
Lasiurus cinereus

Silver-haired Bat pg. 91
Lasionycteris noctivagans

Townsend's Big-eared Bat pg. 91
Corynorhinus townsendii

Spotted Bat pg. 91
Euderma maculatum

Allen's Big-eared Bat pg. 91
Idionycteris phyllotis

Marsupial

Virginia Opossum pg. 263
Didelphis virginiana

Box colors match the
corresponding section of the book.

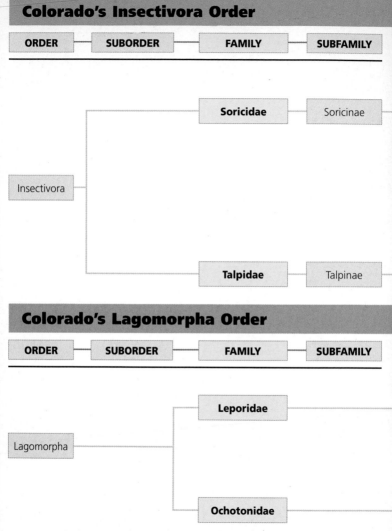

Colorado's Insectivora Order

ORDER	SUBORDER	FAMILY	SUBFAMILY

Insectivora

Soricidae — Soricinae

Talpidae — Talpinae

Colorado's Lagomorpha Order

ORDER	SUBORDER	FAMILY	SUBFAMILY

Lagomorpha

Leporidae

Ochotonidae

Shrews and Mole

Least Shrew pg. 39
Cryptotis parva

Masked Shrew pg. 35
Sorex cinereus

Pygmy Shrew pg. 39
Sorex hoyi

Dwarf Shrew pg. 39
Sorex nanus

Merriam's Shrew pg. 39
Sorex merriami

Montane Shrew pg. 39
Sorex monticolus

Water Shrew pg. 39
Sorex palustris

Desert Shrew pg. 39
Notiosorex crawfordi

Eastern Mole pg. 41
Scalopus aquaticus

Pika, Rabbits and Hares

Mountain Cottontail pg. 183
Sylvilagus nuttallii

Desert Cottontail pg. 187
Sylvilagus audubonii

Eastern Cottontail pg. 191
Sylvilagus floridanus

Snowshoe Hare pg. 195
Lepus americanus

Black-tailed Jackrabbit pg. 199
Lepus californicus

White-tailed Jackrabbit pg. 203
Lepus townsendii

American Pika pg. 179
Ochotona princeps

Box colors match the
corresponding section of the book.

Colorado's Rodentia Order

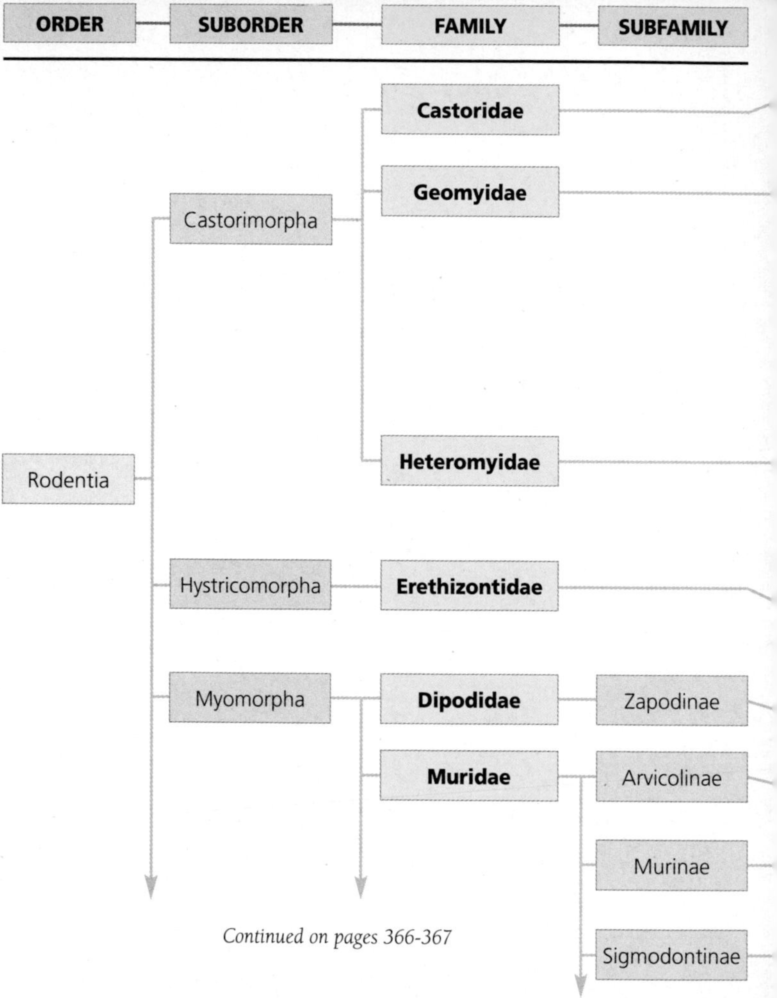

ORDER	SUBORDER	FAMILY	SUBFAMILY

Castoridae

Geomyidae

Castorimorpha

Heteromyidae

Rodentia

Hystricomorpha — **Erethizontidae**

Myomorpha — **Dipodidae** — Zapodinae

Muridae — Arvicolinae

Murinae

Sigmodontinae

Continued on pages 366-367

Rodents

American Beaver pg. 83
Castor canadensis

Botta's Pocket Gopher pg. 177
Thomomys bottae

Northern Pocket Gopher pg. 173
Thomomys talpoides

Yellow-faced Pocket Gopher pg. 177
Cratogeomys castanops

Plains Pocket Gopher pg. 173
Geomys bursarius

Plains Pocket Mouse pg. 45
Perognathus flavescens

Silky Pocket Mouse pg. 49
Perognathus flavus

Olive-backed Pocket Mouse pg. 49
Perognathus fasciatus

Great Basin Pocket Mouse pg. 49
Perognathus parvus

Hispid Pocket Mouse pg. 49
Chaetodipus hispidus

Ord's Kangaroo Rat pg. 71
Dipodomys ordii

North American Porcupine pg. 259
Erethizon dorsatum

Meadow Jumping Mouse pg. 59
Zapus hudsonius

Western Jumping Mouse pg. 57
Zapus princeps

House Mouse pg. 54
Mus musculus

Norway Rat pg. 67
Rattus norvegicus

Southern Red-backed Vole pg. 73
Clethrionomys gapperi

Sagebrush Vole pg. 77
Lemmiscus curtatus

Meadow Vole pg. 77
Microtus pennsylvanicus

Prairie Vole pg. 77
Microtus ochrogaster

Mexican Vole pg. 77
Microtus mexicanus

Montane Vole pg. 77
Microtus montanus

Long-tailed Vole pg. 77
Microtus longicaudus

Heather Vole pg. 77
Phenacomys intermedius

Muskrat pg. 79
Ondatra zibethicus

Hispid Cotton Rat pg. 71
Sigmodon hispidus

Western Harvest Mouse pg. 54
Reithrodontomys megalotis

Plains Harvest Mouse pg. 55
Reithrodontomys montanus

White-footed Mouse pg. 54
Peromyscus leucopus

Deer Mouse pg. 51
Peromyscus maniculatus

Pinyon Mouse pg. 54
Peromyscus truei

Canyon Mouse pg. 55
Peromyscus crinitus

Northern Rock Mouse pg. 55
Peromyscus nasutus

Brush Mouse pg. 55
Peromyscus boylii

Box colors match the
corresponding section of the book.

Colorado's Rodentia Order

ORDER	SUBORDER	FAMILY	SUBFAMILY

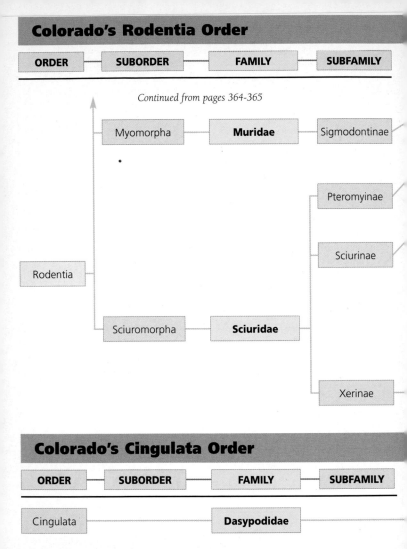

Continued from pages 364-365

Rodentia

- Myomorpha — **Muridae** — Sigmodontinae

- Sciuromorpha — **Sciuridae** — Pteromyinae
  - Sciurinae
  - Xerinae

Colorado's Cingulata Order

ORDER	SUBORDER	FAMILY	SUBFAMILY

Cingulata ——————— **Dasypodidae** ———————

Rodents

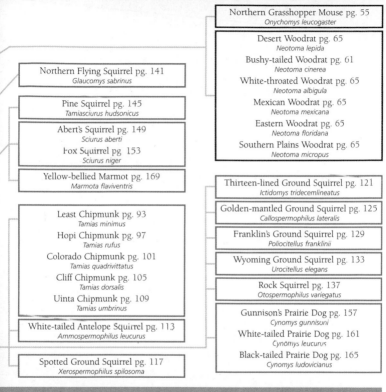

Northern Grasshopper Mouse pg. 55
Onychomys leucogaster

Desert Woodrat pg. 65
Neotoma lepida

Bushy-tailed Woodrat pg. 61
Neotoma cinerea

White-throated Woodrat pg. 65
Neotoma albigula

Mexican Woodrat pg. 65
Neotoma mexicana

Eastern Woodrat pg. 65
Neotoma floridana

Southern Plains Woodrat pg. 65
Neotoma micropus

Northern Flying Squirrel pg. 141
Glaucomys sabrinus

Pine Squirrel pg. 145
Tamiasciurus hudsonicus

Abert's Squirrel pg. 149
Sciurus aberti

Fox Squirrel pg. 153
Sciurus niger

Yellow-bellied Marmot pg. 169
Marmota flaviventris

Thirteen-lined Ground Squirrel pg. 121
Ictidomys tridecemlineatus

Golden-mantled Ground Squirrel pg. 125
Callospermophilus lateralis

Franklin's Ground Squirrel pg. 129
Poliocitellus franklinii

Wyoming Ground Squirrel pg. 133
Urocitellus elegans

Rock Squirrel pg. 137
Otospermophilus variegatus

Least Chipmunk pg. 93
Tamias minimus

Hopi Chipmunk pg. 97
Tamias rufus

Colorado Chipmunk pg. 101
Tamias quadrivittatus

Cliff Chipmunk pg. 105
Tamias dorsalis

Uinta Chipmunk pg. 109
Tamias umbrinus

Gunnison's Prairie Dog pg. 157
Cynomys gunnisoni

White-tailed Prairie Dog pg. 161
Cynomys leucurus

Black-tailed Prairie Dog pg. 165
Cynomys ludovicianus

White-tailed Antelope Squirrel pg. 113
Ammospermophilus leucurus

Spotted Ground Squirrel pg. 117
Xerospermophilus spilosoma

Armadillo

Nine-banded Armadillo pg. 255
Dasypus novemcinctus

Box colors match the
corresponding section of the book.

CHECKLIST/INDEX BY SPECIES

Use the boxes to check the mammals you've seen.

ABOUT THE AUTHOR

Naturalist, wildlife photographer and writer Stan Tekiela is the originator of the popular state-specific field guide series that includes *Birds of Colorado Field Guide*. Stan has authored more than 190 educational books, including field guides, quick guides, nature books, children's books, playing cards and more, presenting many species of animals and plants.

With a Bachelor of Science degree in Natural History from the University of Minnesota and as an active professional naturalist for more than 30 years, Stan studies and photographs wildlife throughout the United States and Canada. He has received various national and regional awards for his books and photographs. Also a well-known columnist and radio personality, his syndicated column appears in more than 25 newspapers, and his wildlife programs are broadcast on a number of Midwest radio stations. Stan can be followed on Facebook and Twitter. He can be contacted via www.naturesmart.com.